"I am not contained in the heavens and the earth.
Yet I can come into the heart of a believer,,,,,"

"I become his hearing with which he hears,
I become his eyes with which he sees,
I become his hands with which he strikes or works
I become his feet with which he walks (and in one tradition),
I become his tongue with which he speaks."

"Young man, (Abne Abbas) I shall teach you some words
(of advice). Be conscious of God, and God will protect you.
Be conscious of God,and you will find Him in front of you."

"Whichever direction you turn, you will find the blessed Face of God."
"I am with you wherever you maybe."

THE BLESSED FACE OF GOD

Is Always Close to You

Love is the life force of the universe
Unleash your true Self

You can revolutionize your life through knowing God.
You can realize your life's full potential through loving God.
You can achieve happiness, inner peace, joy, health and your best life

By Mohammad Afzal Mughal

Copyright © 2012 Inspire Publishing USA Inc.
All rights reserved.

Printed in the United States
by CreateSpace, an Amazon.com Company

Published by Inspire Publishing USA Inc.
www.spiritualbksstore.com
Available at www.createspace.com/3512670

ISBN: 0615474683
ISBN-13: 9780615474687
Library of Congress Control Number - 2011926906
Inspire Publishing USA Inc., Florida, USA

Preface

Imagine this tiny dot is the universe.

●

You, I and billions of our fellow human beings exist in this **dot** along with galaxies, stars, planets, mountains, oceans and lava in the belly of the earth, which the earth throws up occasionally.

The Creator of this dot wants all human beings to live in harmony, compassion, peace, joy, tolerance and love like one family. The earth can become a paradise for you. The best way to achieve that goal is through experiencing closeness to the blessed Face of God. That is the noblest goal which requires developing knowledge, love, focus and self-control.

There is another universe within, which has not yet been discovered. We will share the knowledge of this universe with you throughout this book. This universe is vaster than the outer universe. Perhaps you have never thought of exploring the universe within. I invite you to join me in this spiritual journey through the sacred soul and the loving heart. The most beloved Creator, who is everywhere, can come into the heart, when the heart is purified and saturated with His love.

The Creator of the inner and outer universe is called by many names, most commonly by the names of God, Allah, and Yahweh.

You will be able to feel the presence of the blessed Face of God everywhere through contemplation and while reading this book. To gain maximum benefit, this book should be read with good intention and an open mind. One should strive to:

- Know God
- Create intense love and longing in your heart for God
- Transform your self (ego) into contented self
- Develop patience, friendship and closeness

When the self is purified and contented, it can be molded to have a capacity for seeing and experiencing the spiritual visions. You start comprehending the languages of other creations such as birds, plants and animals. There is nothing in this universe that does not have a meaning and a purpose. Every creation has been bestowed with the ability to think and communicate.

The self cannot envision things of the spiritual world when it is in the grip of fear, worry, pain, greed, and completely engrossed in the material world. It is like a piece of iron ore that needs to be burned in the fire, hammered, and finally molded into a shining sword. The self cannot gain access to the palace of King of kings without going through intense fire of love and passion. All the King asks for are love and devotion.

Let me introduce you to your Loving Creator

Let me introduce you to your loving Creator in an effort to help you know who He really is. You can revolutionize your life positively when you really know Him and experience His blessed Face everywhere. You can achieve your life's full potential by discovering the true reality and purpose. You can invest your time to gain 'the true wealth which is the good you do in this world' said the Prophet Muhammad. The material wealth will follow you anyway. Striving for the material world alone can be like a mirage which will tire and exhaust you. But when you come close to the Beloved of all creations, you will feel as if you own the whole world. You will then be able to feel the state of paradise in this world.

When you become conscious of the greatest source of help, friendship, wisdom, love, healing and compassion, you will have achieved true satisfaction, happiness, and success. You will be inspired to intensify your love of God and transform your life completely. He has created you out of His love for you, you just need to become conscious and purify your heart, so that it can become a mirror which reflects the perfection and beauty of God.

After many years of struggle, learning, and improvements, (this book can help make the journey easier for you) research, guidance from spiritual teachers, contemplation, remembrance, prayers, and patience, I have been able to discover, feel and experience the presence of the blessed Face of God everywhere. This spiritual experience has revolutionized my life significantly so that I can be of service to others and help them experience this reality. I have been able to receive answers to my questions and thoughts through visions, dreams and other channels. Thus I found out how God knows even my hidden thoughts.

Now I feel compelled to share these experiences, knowledge, and wisdom with my fellow human beings through this book. I believe this knowledge can help millions of people prosper spiritually, materially and help them avoid calamities. When you are able to achieve closeness to God, solutions to every challenge in this world are inspired in you.

One thing unique about this book is that it does not teach you thousands of years old teachings but the most advanced and simple, knowledge and inspirations from the Most Wise and the Loving One.

Some people have become billionaires or leaders of great institutions occupying the most prestigious positions, and have achieved their lives' goals. In history, many great leaders conquered lands, built huge, powerful empires, and accumulated great wealth, but then came a time when they had to give up everything against their wishes. You can become the greatest scientist, doctor, or inventor and achieve all the fame and wealth in this world. This reputation and wealth will not remain with you forever. The world is quick to forget the famous and wealthy.

In fact, you will have attained your true potential when you discover the hidden power within you that can help you excel in all aspects of your life. The truly wise focus and gain knowledge, awareness, and relationship with their loving Creator who provides them with maximum happiness, contentment, and inner peace as if lighting up a lamp in their heart that keeps on giving the light and the energy forever.

Love of God, excellent character, generosity, compassion, humility, forgiveness, service and love toward all human beings can become the true wealth in your life. This investment grows forever.

This book is an effort to share knowledge that can inspire you to experience the presence of the Blessed Face of God. You can gradually develop a loving relationship with your Creator and find in Him the best friend you ever had. You can reflect on the beauty, majesty, mercy, and the compassion of God who created all these wonderful miracles that we see around us.

Abraham, Moses, Jesus and Muhammad and other messengers are in the presence of God in paradise at this very moment. God sent them, at different times, to teach the straight path of life and set models for all human beings to attain love and closeness to God. In one tradition, the Prophet Muhammad said that one hour's contemplation is superior to eighty years of worship. Contemplation in God accelerates your spiritual progress. That does not mean to lower the value of worship but to show the greater value of contemplation in God. The spiritual contemplation can bring in a true spiritual revolution in your life.

We have the freedom of choice whether to believe in God or disbelieve or to be grateful to Him or be ungrateful. The entire human race can choose to live in complete harmony and joy in the presence of their appreciating Creator but because of a lack of knowledge, poverty, and ignorance, billions of lives are just drifting on the ocean of darkness. Our positive choices and focus can create consciousness and love in our lives. We can spread the light all over and contribute towards world peace. We can learn to live in harmony, tolerance and joy.

As you read this book, you will experience inspirations and awakenings. Seize the moment and initiate the spiritual journey by inspiring yourself and becoming conscious of the blessed Face of God.

Everything in this book is equally useful and applicable to both genders, but the masculine gender is used as the default throughout the book.

This book is based on study, research, inspirations and thousands of practical experiences. Some people might think that this writing is a figment of my imagination, but it is not the case. We have been led to believe that God is outside the universe or very far in the heavens above and beyond. We look above to see if God is up there not knowing what we consider to be up might, in fact, be down as the earth is floating. His words are an ocean of knowledge, wisdom and the truth. It is worth mentioning some of the verses which fuelled my passion for seeking the blessed Face of God.

It is clear that God wants us to know that His blessed Face is in every direction to which we turn our faces. There is no place in the universe where He is not present.

Whatsoever direction you turn, there is the Face of God.

"And to God belongs the East and the West, so whichever direction you turn; there is the Face of God. Surely, God is All-Sufficient and All-Knowing." [1]

God is closer to us than our jugular veins.

"And We are nearer to him than his jugular veins." [2]

Everything in existence will perish save the blessed Face of God.

"Everything in existence will perish..."
"And the Face of Your Lord full of Majesty and Honor will remain forever." [3]

I am very close to them.

"If they ask you (the Prophet) about Me, I am very close to them, I answer their prayer..." [4]

God is with you wherever you may be.

"Have you not seen that God knows whatsoever is in the heavens, and whatsoever is on the earth? There is not a secret meeting of three but He is the Fourth, nor of five but He is the sixth — Nor between fewer nor more, But He is with them ... Verily, God has full knowledge of everything" [5]

Seeking His Face.

"Be Patient with those who call their Lord God morning and evening, seeking The Face of God."[6]

Those who will strive in Us

"And those who will strive in Us (God) the paths (of light and guidance) will be opened for them. God is with those who worship Him as if they see Him."[7]

By constantly stating about His blessed Face, God wants us to strive, contemplate, love and become closer to Him. When you start this spiritual journey, He keeps opening the doors for you to know Him better and become conscious of His presence. You can discover it through personal experience.

I hope that by the time you have been through this book, you will be able to develop a special love in your heart for God and your life will be transformed positively. You remember Him, He will remember you. You love Him, He too will love you. God knows you and sees you even this moment. Your life will start experiencing a spiritual revolution and you will be able to realize your life's full potential. The true success is when you have achieved your life's goals materially and spiritually.

Mohammad Afzal Mughal
Florida, July 2012

Table of Contents

Table of Contents

1

The Blessed
Face of God

is always So Close to You

"And to God Belong the East and the West, to whichever direction you turn, there is the Face of God. Surely! God is All-Sufficient and All-Knowing."[8]

God is declaring to us that when we focus on Him, we can feel the presence of His blessed Face. Should you turn your face toward the east, west, north, south, heavens above, or deep within your heart, you can feel God's presence. When we develop God's love in our hearts, we will feel the presence of His Blessed Face.

When God's existence is questioned, then it is not possible to feel His Blessed Face. If you don't believe in the existence of paradise, you would not be able to enter it as belief in God is the key.

Conversely, we can seek and develop the spiritual eyes within us, which can enable us to experience the presence of the blessed Face of God. You can feel His presence everywhere when you strive to seek Him. The information given in this book can help you become aware of His Presence.

The Time is Now. This Moment is for you to Fall in Love

The time is now. This moment is for you to fall in love with the One who loves you the most in the universe. How long will you continue ignoring His presence and love for you.

How can God be everywhere?

About twelve hundred years ago in Baghdad, a great scholar named Abu Hanifa was asked by his students to explain how God can be everywhere. He was a man of knowledge and wisdom. Instead of giving a long lecture, he simply asked his students to bring candles. In the pitch dark room, he asked that the candles be lit. The light from these candles spread all over the room. He explained to them that the way the light from these candles spread to each part of the room is how God's light and presence is everywhere in the universe as expressed in the verse: "God is the Light of the Heavens and the earth."

Every Face Turns toward Your Face

You show your Face
In every particle (atom)
You've become
The shining sun
From every direction
Present in Kaaba and present in monastery
Every Face
Turns toward your own (Face)

You are the destination
Of believers
And nonbelievers.

Tabib Shirazi

You are breathing His sacred breath

God created the first human being, Adam, out of water and clay. God says:

> *"When I created Adam, I breathed into him My Spirit and he became alive."*[9]

Do you realize that you are breathing the same breath that God breathed into Adam and thereby starting the chain of humanity? It is clear that we, all human beings, were created as the best creation of God, and we did not evolve from animals as espoused by some scientists.

Our Evolution is: We have progressed from animal behavior to human behavior

God kept all the animals to this day to ensure the truth. We used to live and behave like animals. Our evolution is that we have become so much civilized progressing from the animal life to superior human life. But animals have always lived civilized life as they don't kill any other animal unless they are hungry. However, we have regressed to even lower than animal behavior as we have killed our innocent fellow human beings in hundreds, thousands and millions.

You, the greatest living miracle.

Study your physical life, each part of your body and each organ. Just concentrate on your breathing, hear your heartbeat or feel your pulse, you will come to know that you are the greatest miracle on this earth and God is the originator, designer, creator, and sustainer.

Your breathing is the proof of His existence, presence, and creative power just like a beautiful garden is the proof of the gardener's attention and care of its flowers, plants and trees.

You can find refuge and peace in God.

"Every living and moving creatures' forelock is in His Hand."[10]

God does not refuse anyone who wishes to take refuge in Him or seek faith from Him. There is no person, place, or space in the universe that is hidden from the presence and the sight of the Almighty God. Who can give refuge and peace when one finds all doors closed? It is only God whose doors are always open unconditionally for His creation. He is always waiting for us to turn to Him with devotion as He says:

"Oh man! What is stopping you from coming close to your Generous Lord." [11]

He even takes care of those who deny His existence.

Everything in the heavens and on the earth glorifies, celebrates, and praises God, but only a few members of mankind really love, thank, remember and appreciate Him.

No other creation denies the presence of God except some who say that nature created everything and when you ask them who created the nature, they have no answer. It is clear that nothing in this universe can create itself.

However, millions of people all over the world are complaining and are ungrateful, and rebellious to God. The rebellion is so serious that, right in His presence, many people openly declare, "There is no God" yet He tolerates and protects them which proves that He is merciful to all mankind.

It is always this Moment, no past and future in the sight of God

There is no past and future in the sight of God; it is always the present moment. We do live in the past, the present, and the future, but God is beyond the limitations of space and time. For Him, it is always this moment. The seeker of His blessed Face finds himself living in the present moment, enjoying His Presence now.

God's Presence is Here and Now. This very Moment.

The action of thinking about the past and the future steals your time which is your life. Stop thinking of the past and future. Become wise and live in the Presence of God now as He is here and now.

The Vision of Your Face

Your love, from before
The beginning of time,
Is my soul
It's my very self.

Your love is the treasure
Of my weak, begging heart.

Perhaps your beauty
Has been far from me
But the Vision
Of your Face
Has stayed with me always

Sultan Walad

He is directing the affairs of the universe each day

He creates everything in complete silence. Millions of human beings are born all over the world every day. New islands are emerging and the earth is undergoing change each day. This creation and recreation is going on in total silence from the beginning of time. The Everlasting One is directing the affairs of the universe according to His wish and plan. He is tolerant and patient with His creatures. That shows the **true greatness of God.**

2

The Beauty of His Blessed Face

**One cannot bear to see the infinite beauty
It has been kept invisible.**

His beauty exceeds all the beauties of the universe which cannot explain the majestic, glory and the beauty of His blessed Face.

Wherever you see beauty, it is the reflection of the glimpse of the Most Beautiful.

The universe is the manifestation of God's perfect attributes.

The beautiful waterfalls, sunsets, rainbows, heavens above, artistic clouds, the colors of the butterflies, tulips, roses, and flowers all symbolize and represent the wonders of God.

"Verily, God is the Most Beautiful and He loves beauty." [12]

God has not created anything which is not beautiful but we fail to perceive and reflect. He always inspires us to see the beauty and splendor in the universe.

In Rumi's words:

If you want the witness of heaven to show Himself, make your heart the companion of a mirror-polishing file!

Make the house of your body a garden and rosary! Make the corner of your heart a mosque or a chapel

Oh, if only you would open the door of this house for an instant, you would see that the heart of every existent thing is your intimate friend.

He would show His Face and say,

"I am your witness, fear not! Think not of loss, for you have found gain. God has disclosed all things, fresh and withered, but He has sealed the spirit's mysteries by saying - from the command of thy Lord.

The Beauty of Your Face

Over hundreds of axons,
Creation's fabric
Unfolded
Until the **beauty**
Of **Your Face**
Blazed forth
In this world

From the top of your head
To the tip of your toe
Glory to God
All praise belongs to God

Miraculously
He has molded you
To my very desire

Khaqani Shirwan

The eye does not see anything except God!

Vision of the Beloved is the true capital of love.

Once the seeker is given the slightest taste of vision's ecstasy, the fire in his heart will blaze up, and he can totally lose interest in everything other than God.

"Every day He is upon a task." [13]

He displays a hundred colors at every instant, for every day God is in full control of the universe.

If He were to show Himself in a thousand appearances, none of them would ever resemble any other. In His effects and acts every instant you see something different because none of His acts resemble any other. Each manifestation of His essence is also different.

You can see God at this very moment through His manifestations in everything existing

Everything you see around is declaring:

"I have been created by God. He is my Creator. I am the proof of His existence and presence. He is everywhere. He is ensuring my sustenance and survival every moment. He is the source of my creation and my end. He has created means but He is hidden behind everything."

Your Face

When I drew near
To the candle of your Face
I became plaintive and daring
Just like the moth.

On the day I'm released
From this miserable cage
Like the king's royal falcon
I'll fly free at last.

Khwaja Abdallah Ansari

3

The Light of God's Blessed Face

God is the Light of the Heavens and the Earth.[14]

The divine energy from His light caused the big bang. The universe was created and has been evolving ever since. Billions of years later, scientists continue to study the big bang and assume theories based on their research. The light is only one of the ninety-nine attributes of God. These ninety-nine attributes are a summary of His infinite attributes. The blessed Face of God is beyond the layers of infinite light upon light. There are so many lights of different colors in the universe, and scientists have discovered the existence of dark energy in the space not to mention white or colorless energy.

His light illuminates everything in the universe.

God's light brought existence out of the sphere of nonexistence.

He provides divine light and is the source of all light in the entire universe and to the faces, minds, and hearts of those seeking and longing for His blessed Face. God is the light that is shone upon the whole creation—the sun, the moon, the stars, and the galaxies—making it clearly visible. Wherever there is light, that is from His light.

He guides to his light those whom He loves.

Those who have not been given light by God, have no light. Of course, it's their choice. They can open their hearts to receive the light now, or they can choose to remain without it. If you wish to advance and excel on the path of love, and make God the goal of your life, He has promised to guide you. He does not compel anyone. Whoever knocks at His door, the way will be opened for him.

The Infinite Light

There is light that is visible to the human eye, and there is light that can be seen only by the scientific instruments which can spot the particles of light and energy. The eyes of the purified heart can see the presence of God's light, which shines on everything in existence. His light is pure white light and has different colors like a rainbow. His light can show any color and all colors.

God's Light

If someone's always been steeped
In the Presence of God
For such a soul
The king is like a beggar
And the beggar is like a king.

In the faces of people
Such a saint
Sees God's Light

Yes—human beings (annihilated in the love of God)
Like a mirror, Can reflect the Face of God!

Kabi Kabuli

His light is shining on the sun, which is the source of solar energy. His light creates energy, lightening and thunder. It brightens the mother's womb for the tiny baby. His light causes the balancing act in the oceans, snow, and water. His energy creates new islands and human beings each moment.

His messengers and seekers on the path of light.

God illuminated the hearts of His special messengers like Abraham, Moses, Jesus, and Muhammad whom He sent to guide mankind. Some people listened to these messengers and became believers, but the others opposed them and even denied the existence of God. The messengers' hearts were filled with the light from God, and they further tried to spread God's light to all mankind. Afterward, the spiritual teachers continued to persuade people to surrender and love God. Some people have made the choice to know and feel His presence while in this world. They will see the truth in afterlife and will be pleased beyond their imagination. But those, who choose to deny the existence of God in this world, will be surprised to see His presence in the next world

He is still illuminating the hearts of those who are seeking His blessed Face. You, too, can become a seeker and ignite the light in your heart and in the world.

The light of faith decorates the hearts.

God has bestowed on us the light of faith which shows us the straight path of peace and salvation. It gives the believer an enlightened face and excellent character thus eliminating the darkness of disbelief and sin.

Without Your Face

You are like the sun
Come!
Without your Face, the garden is yellow and pale
Come!
Without you, the world is like dust
Come!
Without you, the circle of love turns cold.
Come!

Rumi

God has hidden the light of faith in the hearts of those men and women who love Him. There is visible light which we can see and there is an invisible light which is finer and we are unable to see. The Angels are made of finer pure light and are invisible to our sight.

You can be linked to this source of light and be energized. Faith is like a lamp you carry with you to guide your way in life. This lamp can open the door to the house of God and allow you to draw near Him, Who is the light of the heavens and the earth.

4

God is the Source
of All Energy

The Light upon Light... [15]

Light, which emanates from the blessed Face of God, enables each atom and cell to live, and function. Similarly, the entire universe performs its functions assigned to it by the creator God through the energy it receives from His light. No man's intelligence, vision, or imagination can measure the greatness of God.

The devil and one's own ego suggest negative thoughts to keep one in darkness and away from the infinite light. The devil will not be able to enter the heart illuminated by the light of faith. The door to the heart is the mind, and the light of that door is knowledge. It blocks out the evil of ignorance, hypocrisy, and arrogance.

Light or energy lifts you up and darkness takes you down

The life starts with the light from the loving Creator.
Light is life and darkness is nonexistence.
Light lifts you up and darkness brings you down.
Light is wisdom and knowledge, but darkness is ignorance.
Light is belief and darkness is disbelief.
Light is love and darkness is hatred.
Light is surrender and darkness is arrogance.
Light is humility and darkness is false pride and boasting.
Light is faith and darkness is rebellion.
Light is acceptance and darkness is refusal.
Light is truth and darkness is lies.
Light is beauty and darkness is confusion.
Light is honesty and darkness is fraud.
Light is hope and darkness is despair.

You Are the Light

You are the **King**
And have checkmated
Every beautiful soul.

You are the **Sun**
The rest are your atoms.

You are the **Light**
Every creation
Is your lamp

You are the **Essence**
The entire world
Is your living sign.

Tuti Hamadani

God's light is the pure energy creating all movement.

The lava hidden in the depths of the mountains moves because of the divine energy, which also makes hearts beat, blood circulate, and maintain the rhythm of inhalation and exhalation. The eyes, ears, each organ and every cell in the body are alive and function because of the energy from His light.

Light can make the darkness disappear.

Wherever you see any light it points to its source. Every leaf moving is expressing its love for the Creator. Every cloud that moves is expressing its love for the light of all lights. Every wave that dances is showing its appreciation for its Creator. Oceans glorify His beauty and majesty. All celestial bodies move in ecstasy because of a longing for Him

Only a few human beings feel ecstasy because of uncontrollable love for their Beloved. The majority don't have that ecstatic feeling.

The entire universe would be in total darkness and nothing could exist in the darkness without the perfect light emanating from the blessed Face of God. There will be no motion, no action, and no existence of the living bodies in the total darkness. Imagine yourself living in the layers of darkness like the bottom of an ocean.

Every atom points to its Creator.

The sun receives the light from the divine light. The sun shines light on the sky and the earth, enabling us to see things around us. This light enables us to identify what is beneficial and what is harmful. In the light we find our way and guidance for our lives. The sun is simply doing its job assigned to it by its Creator who is also sustaining it through continuous energy.

The Moon reflects light from the Sun

The moon and stars don't have the light of their own but reflect light from the sun and have been providing guidance to the traveling caravans and ships in the oceans since the ancient times.

Even the blind believe in God and love Him.

The blind can see things through the invisible light of faith. You can come across people who are blind and never seen anything in this world, but they believe firmly in God. But some people with sight find it difficult to perceive the presence of God everywhere.

It is easier for the blind person to believe in God because he can feel and perceive His presence within unlike many human beings who have been completely overtaken by the material world and can hardly see and feel the presence of the true owner and controller of the universe.

The scientist cannot observe the invisible light in the universe through scientific experiments. The only way he would be able to see and feel the presence of this light is through spiritual experiments and results.

The Light of Thy Face

"I seek refuge in the Light of Thy Noble Face on whose account the Heavens and the earth lighted, the depths of darkness shined, and the affairs of this world and the next world were organized and ordered well..." Supplication of the Prophet Muhammad

The World Is a Veil on the Face of Our Friend

A Mirage
The world is a veil
On the face of our Friend

The world is a bubble
In the sea of His existence

In the sight of those greedy for the Wearer of Being,
The world is a mirage in the desert of seeking.

Muhammad Shirin Maghribi

O' My Lord God, cover me completely with Thy light

"O' God, place light in my heart, light on my face, light in my chest, light in front of me, light behind me, light on my right, light on my left, light above me, light below me, light in my hearing, light in my eyesight, light on my forehead, Light in my hair, light in my skin, light in my flesh, light in my blood, light in my bones; O' God, saturate me with abundant light and cover me completely in Thy light." [16]

"God is the light of the heavens and the earth." [17]

He knows that all existence, knowledge, thought, and feeling come from that light, and all existence and knowledge in the universe are nothing but the manifestation of that light.

Angels are made of finer light that is invisible to our eyes.

Angels live in the presence of God. They can perceive the might and power of God; hence, they are always in a state of awe, love, and prostration. They do not perform functions for receiving reward but do things out of love. They are always glorifying and singing the praises of God and fulfilling their duties in total obedience. They never disobey their Creator unlike us human beings.

> God says:"there is not a soul on whom We have not appointed angels for protection until the appointed time."[18]

Distance to the Beloved Only One Step

Taste the music
In the lover's sigh

Discover the cure
In yearning's pain.

The distance
To the Beloved
Is only one step

Why not, then,
Take that step?

Baba Al Din Muhammad Amili

5

God is the Most Loving

God is the source of infinite love.

If God loves you, the entire universe loves you.

"And yet there are some people, who replace God with rivals, loving them as God should be loved. But the believers love God intensely."[19]

The attribute of Love means God loves all creatures intensely. The word love cannot sufficiently express the meaning of extreme and intense love that is Al-Wadud, the most loving one. God is the ocean of Love.

God has special love for His good servants. He is the only One who is worthy of passionate love. He must be loved and adored by everyone as life is a gift and every breath is a favor from Him. God in His infinite and unconditional love has implanted in the hearts of His good servants intense love for Himself and for all human beings. He has given them the vision to give and receive love and be truthful.

When faith is intensified with love and put into action, it becomes devotion which creates enlightenment.

The more you know God, the more you love Him

The heart of the good servant seeks God's love. But love is only possible if the lover is aware of the beloved, as well as the beauty and perfection of the beloved. How can one appreciate the beloved without the true knowledge of Him? Strive to achieve knowledge and love of God. The more you know Him, the more passionately you will love Him. This relationship can create closeness and friendship which is hard to explain and which continues growing.

All creatures love God intensely.

He is and should be the object of love, adoration, worship, praise, songs, and prayers by every visible and invisible creation. He is the object of submission by all religions, tribes, and nations. People can find consolation in obedience and prostration to Him.

Who Dwells in the Beloved's Presence?

Those who dwell
In the Beloved's presence
Don't obsess on His thought
And speak of Him
Even less

But those who huff and howl
Like the bellows of a bagpipe,
Call for him in a loud voice
Because they are far away.

Baba Afzal Kashani

You will love for others that which you love for yourself.

When you have attained love of God, then you will love for other people that which you love for yourself. Indeed, you will put the needs of others before your own needs because of the state of positive love in your heart. You will see Who is close to you and close to your fellow human beings. God created you as well as those who hold animosity towards you. He is the Lord of all creations. He has planted love in our hearts and you can see this love being displayed by parents, children, spouses, relatives, friends every day all over the world.

Love inspires you to sacrifice your needs for others.

It is in man's nature to strive for his personal survival, needs, success, and safety. How can he sacrifice his own needs and goals for others? It is unimaginable. But when one is inspired through the fuel of love of God, he can sacrifice his own needs for the happiness and joy of others.

> *Even when one suffers at the hands of those for whom one wishes more than one wishes for himself, one should react as did the Prophet Muhammad. When persecuted by pagans who put a price on his head, he migrated from the city of his birth to the distant city of Medina. He then had no choice but to defend himself, and when wounded in the battle and bleeding, instead of saying Oh! God, destroy these people waging war*

against me, he said:"O my Lord, guide my people as they do not know the Truth."[20]

Due to their not having the true information because of a screen over their eyes caused by their hatred, they might not have acted this way. They wanted to kill him just because he was calling them to worship and love the One and only God instead of hundreds of idols. He felt pity for them. The result of his prayer was that many of those archenemies became his supporters and close friends.

God can love you beyond your imagination.

You should nourish the flame of love in your heart, and God can purify your heart and perfect your character. When God loves His servant, He spreads the love for that servant far and wide, so that almost everyone in the world loves him too as explained in the tradition below:

> *When God loves a servant He calls the archangel Gabriel and says,"I love this servant of mine, you love him also."Then Gabriel calls unto angels in the heavens and says, "Oh all those who are in the heavens, God loves this servant, you love him too."This announcement reaches to the angels of the lower heavens and, in turn, they too love that person. So all that exists in the heavens love him. Then the love of that servant is announced to the creatures of the earth including human beings and they love him also.* [21]

6

Love or Ishq can Revolutionize Your Life

Ishq can spiritually inflame your Soul

It is a Dynamic Force

Love or the Ishq is the fastest vehicle for self-transformation and it transcends everything else in the entire universe. When you become conscious of the presence of the blessed Face of God, you will find everything in the universe functioning because of His love.

Heart is the instrument of Love, Dynamic Force with no dimension

Ahmed Ghazzali, a spiritual scholar, views love as a phenomenon having no dimension; he further relates that just as eyes are for seeing and ears for hearing, the heart is the instrument of love, and if one does not utilize it, the loss is like not using one's eyes and brain. A heart without an object of desire is a man without a goal and he feels restless. As soon as he falls in love, he finds himself in a state of 'intimacy' and an acceptance of the world. The nature of 'love', is beyond limitation of thinking and ordinary science. Through ordinary science we can reach the shore, but 'love' is diving into the ocean. Then our ordinary consciousness is of no assistance.

At the beginning, the lover is like static energy until, at the proper time, the proper object of desire attracts him. Then his static energy turns into a dynamic force (or Ishq). The direction of this dynamic force is always toward 'Thou' the Beloved God.

All the cells, atoms, and planets revolve around in His love.

The moon and other planets orbiting around the sun are all floating and thus expressing their passion for the center of everything. All the cells, molecules, atoms are revolving around in their intoxication of God's love. Acknowledgement of God's love should be the goal of all creation and the purpose of their being created.

All of God's creations remain in surrender to Him except majority of men

When man loves God and excels all creation in his love, his tears roll down in the emotion of love. He writes poetry and prose to express His love, sings songs of His love and praises.

Love is the Life Force of the Entire Universe

Life's Flame
Love is a source of many great troubles

But lacking love
Is a disgrace
For travelers upon this path

Love is the life force of the entire universe
Those who lack love
Are already (like) dead.

Awad al Din Kirmani

Love is above the laws of the world. Through love God becomes yours and you become His in everlasting friendship.

Nothing is above the law but love is above all laws. God can remove nations for the sake of one whom He loves. Remember how God let the floods destroy the whole world for the one who was denied and mocked at, the Prophet Noah. It is said that he was calling people to the way of God for decades but people became arrogant and persecuted him instead of listening to his simple message. He was constantly praying to God for the guidance of his people.

The great Rumi expresses the wisdom of love so well:

Through love thorns become roses,
Through love vinegar becomes sweet wine,
Through love the stake becomes a thorn,
Through love the reverse of fortune seems good fortune,
Through love a prison seems a rose bower,
Through love a grate full of tasks seems a garden,
Through love a burning fire is a pleasing light,
Through love the devil becomes a houri,
Through love the hard stone becomes soft as butter,
Through love grief is a joy,
Through love ghouls turn into angels,

Through love stings are as honey,
Through love lions are harmless as mice,
Through love sickness is as health,
Through love wrath is as mercy.

God loves

"Those who do good deeds" [23]
"Those who seek His forgiveness and repent."[24]
"Those who purify themselves" [25]
"Those who have fear-love of God" [26]
"Those who are steadfast persevering" [27]
"Those who place their trust in God" [28]
"Those who act justly" [29]
"Those who strive for His purpose" [30]
"Those who follow His Prophet" [31]

Believers love God intensely.

"And there are people who choose objects whom they love as they should love God. But the believers love God intensely." [32]

God says He does not love the aggressors, arrogant, wasteful spenders, evildoers, unjust, those who create mischief on this earth and do not acknowledge His existence or do not believe in Him. [33]

Love is mentioned in all holy scriptures: Torah, Bible and Quran

You will not have faith until you love one another

You will not enter paradise until you have faith, and you will not have faith until you love one another. Do you want me to tell you something you can do to make you love one another? Make it a habit to greet one another with Peace be upon you. [34]

Love can Help You Achieve Your Life's Full Potential.

When God brings you so close to Himself, you have more spiritual power and joy than any king, queen, or leader of a nation. But you do not hurt any creation including human beings

There was a spiritual teacher who loved God intensely and had achieved closeness with God. The king sent a delegation to bring this man to his palace. The delegation asked the spiritual man to accompany them to the king's palace. The man said he had no need or reason to visit the king. When this message reached the king, he felt humiliated and decided to punish the spiritual teacher. He ordered his general to arrest the man and bring him to the court. When the general came to arrest the man and ordered him to come along with them, he told them to go back because your king has been assassinated by one of his top commanders. They turned back in haste and were shocked to find the king had indeed been assassinated. A few years later, the similar incident took place with another arrogant king. The spiritual men desire friendship and closeness to God and wish to serve fellow human beings in humility

The Glow of Your Presence (Face)

The Glow of Your Presence (Face)
Where have you taken your sweet song?
Come back and play me a tune.

I never really cared for the things of this world.
It was the glow of your presence
That filled it with beauty.

Hafiz

My servant draws near to Me until I love him

Almighty God said, "My servant draws near to Me with nothing more loved by Me than the acts of worship that I have enjoined upon him."

My servant continues to draw near to Me with more devotion and additional good works, until I love him or her. When I love him,

I will be his hearing with which he hears,

I will be His sight with which he sees,

I will become his hand with which he strikes (or works)

I will become his feet by which he walks,

When he asks Me for something, I will respond and

When he takes refuge in Me, I will grant it to him......" [35]

Mothers manifest the Loving attribute of God

This love can even be seen in female birds and animals.

Mothers manifest God's loving care for their children and show the best example of loving nature. Mothers normally teach softness like going through adversities with perseverance and never giving up in life while fathers teach toughness and adventures like climbing the mountains of life.

God has ninety-nine times more love for us than our mothers.

"He distributed love—one percent among you all and all His creations and He is still possessing the other ninety-nine percent of all love. So whenever you see an act of love by anyone in this world, that is out of one percent of the love God distributed among all His creation. The rest of ninety-nine percent of the Love will be used on the day of Judgment when He will find the smallest act of goodness to forgive people."[36]

7

God's Invincible Might and Force

He has power over all things. The entire universe is in His hand.

"There is none to reject His Command, none to disobey His decrees."[37]

Water in the oceans can evaporate in seconds, bringing an end to the creatures living in it. If we do not get sufficient rain, we will have drought all over. But it doesn't happen because God has decreed for these systems to be of service to all His creation and, in return, the human beings are supposed to be in service to God and each other.

He has established systems which create hurricanes, twisters, earthquakes, floods, snowstorms, and other natural disasters in the world. New galaxies are being created and so are new islands.

The universe is constantly going through changes and expansion. All these events demonstrate God's invincible might and power.

Lightening travels at speeds of 36000 km/h and can heat the air to 20000 C (36000 F); three times the temperature of the sun's surface

God alone ensures that all the planets in the universe remain in their orbits without any deviation. Consider the power of lightening which can travel at speeds of 36000 km/h and can rapidly heat the air in its immediate vicinity to 20,000 C (36000 F). This is about three times the temperature of the surface of the sun.

Due to advanced technology, you can see a hurricane's eye and, we helplessly watch hurricanes approaching land and causing tremendous devastation. It is as if God is declaring that all human beings can gather together and cannot stop any of the natural disasters that give us fear and hope? We often hear people complaining of drought and then after a few months, we hear complaints of floods.

There are angels in charge of clouds and rain and many other duties. They carry the clouds to where the rain is required for human beings, cattle, and plantation.

Drowned in Your Essence

Drowned in Your Essence
All the world's atoms
Are really your mirrors?
Drowned in your essence
Like drops in the sea.
Like waves that roll over,
Crashing in emptiness,
They deny themselves
They offer your proof

Walah Dahistani

The universe is unveiling and evolving each moment.

God is controlling and is creating and recreating the elements in the universe which is unveiling and evolving with new planets

God does not prevent men from doing voluntary actions by way of acquisition because He created power and is the source of all energy. Actions of man are his possessions; they are nevertheless not outside the will of God.

He is nourishing even the blade of grass and plantation. He is providing us sustenance through rice, barley, wheat, cattle, seafood, vegetables, and fruits. He gives us supply of fresh water.

He is providing ideas and energy to the human minds, ensuring inventions and innovations. He is creating cures of diseases through scientists, physicians, and medicine. It's God's plan to maintain a balance in the universe and ensure that human beings move through life's cycle.

Your Irresistible Glance

With your irresistible glance,
You captured my heart and soul
Having robbed me of those,

Take away my name and accomplishments too
If any trace of me remains in this world
Please, don't delay – take that too.

Ayn al-Qudat Hamadani

What is stopping us from thinking of our Creator?

"O, My servant! What is stopping you from coming close to your Generous Lord?"[38]

Why have we forgotten our Creator who loves us more than anything in the universe? It is sad that we don't even have a few moments to reflect on Him?

God challenges all human beings to create a fly.

All mankind can gather together and still cannot even approach the sun. Our power grinds to a halt before just one of God's creations—the sun, let alone billions of other more powerful planets in the space.

"You all human beings can gather together and cannot create a fly." [39]

If all the human beings gather together, we are unable to create a fly which has a small brain, the nervous system, the eyes to see and persistence and ability to take away particles and germs. She has perfect wings to fly to the roofs or trees. She has a family life and a life cycle. It is obvious that we can never make a small fly that will function as the real fly.

8

God is the Manifest
and the Hidden

He is the open and secret, visible, and invisible.
There is nothing like Him

*"He is the First and the Last, the Manifest and the Hidden
and He is All-Knower of Everything."*[40]

He is the manifest and hidden, first, last, open, and secret. He
is eternal. Unlike human beings, God is without form or shape;
there is nothing like Him. We have length and breadth and height,
but there is no example of God. He is the light of the heavens and
the earth. He has the perfect attributes and qualities.

Everything in the universe is a manifestation
of God's attributes.

He creates, plans, designs, fashions and recreates

God is manifest through His creations like a painter through his paintings. You can feel His presence everywhere. You can also see His presence through the creation taking place all around you each moment.

When you see beautiful hills, lakes, plants, trees, flowers, grass, birds, butterflies, honeybees, the heavens above, stars, day, night, and billions of human beings, you know that their creator is around somewhere. When one sees the wonderful creations all around, one can appreciate the thinker, planner, designer, and fashioner who selected these color combinations, shapes, features, and other elements for each of His creations. You can see the fresh yellow and red roses on bushes where there were only buds a few days earlier. If you consider His perfect creation, you will see God the manifest one and your faith will be complete. The manifest and the hidden are also in man. His form, his words, his actions, and his work are manifest. His intentions, emotions, feelings, and thoughts are hidden.

Only One Light in the Universe

There is naught in the Universe
Save One Light!
One Source of Light!

It appears in a variety of manifestations
God is the Light;
Its manifestation, the Universe

Unification is this;
The rest is illusion and tall talk

Rumi

The Outer and the Inner Universe.

When you close your eyes, focus inward, and contemplate within, you can feel the presence of God. You begin to feel energized and refreshed. He is transcendent through His creative artistry, unparallel beauty, fashion and design. As mentioned previously, we think there is only the outer universe but there is also the universe within man.

Everything around us and above in the heavens is His creation. We have not created anything in the universe but are engaged in probing and discovering the hidden mysteries of the universe. God has given us the creative power to develop and build great machines like spaceships, airplanes, etc.

A Contemplation in God

'I Am with you wherever you maybe'

He is close to us but we are not conscious of His presence

God is the First, and the Last,
The Manifest and the Hidden,
He is seeing and hearing everything.
He is the Knower of all things visible and invisible
He is close to us
He is always in our hearts.
He is transcendent and immanent
He is on His Blessed Throne in the heavens above and yet
everywhere in the universe
His Presence is in the bottom of the oceans taking care of His
creatures He is providing sustenance to creatures in the depth of
the mountains
He is always with us wherever we might be
He is invisible to our eyes but visible to the eyes of the heart
You can feel His Blessed Face so close to you when your heart is
purified to receive pure light.
Each flower,
Each leaf,
Each plant,
Each butterfly silently communicates the reality
Who created it but we do not understand its languages
Birds sing songs of His praise before they go in search of food

He is not far from us and is always near.
But we take ourselves far due to our preoccupation
with the world
He is focused on us due to His love for us
So let's focus on Him with love

9

God is Closer to us than our Jugular Veins

His presence within us beyond any imagination

"We have created human being, and We know what thoughts his self whispers to him. And We are nearer to him than his jugular veins."[41]

God created man and knows his inner desires and motives even better than man himself. He says in the above verse that He is closer to man than his own jugular vein. The jugular vein is the big trunk vein that carries blood from the head to the heart. There are two jugular veins that correspond to the two carotid arteries, which carry the blood from heart to the head.

As the bloodstream is the vehicle of life and consciousness, the phrase, "nearer than the jugular vein" can be interpreted by people according to the level of their faith in God and the level of their knowledge.

God's Knowledge of man's inner most thoughts

The prior verse talks about His knowledge and closeness to us:

"We created man and we know what thoughts go through his self."

God knows more truly the inner most state of our feelings, thoughts, emotions and consciousness than we do.

How is it possible for Him to know our inner thoughts if we think He is too far from us? He speaks the truth that He is so close to us and we must realize it so as to enjoy His friendship and love.

He is closer to us through awareness, knowledge, wisdom and presence. It becomes clear that His closeness to us is beyond any one's comprehension and imagination.

God is closer to us than even our own selves

The second verse has more meaning and we should reflect on it. Man's hearing, seeing, tasting, smelling and speaking faculties have to do with his face and, therefore, lie outside of him.

The Mirror of Your Royal Beauty

The Mirror and Its Case
Each soul is created to serve as your mirror

All things in the two worlds
Are only your mirror

The heart is the mirror of your most royal
Beauty

And both of these worlds
Is the case of that mirror?

Najm al Din Daya Razi

The jugular vein is not outside of our bodies but inside. So God is closer to us than even our own selves. One's closeness to a person is perceived by one's eyesight or feelings. It means that no one can be closer to us than our Creator.

If we realize and become conscious of His closeness, it will not be possible for us to oppress others or be arrogant towards our fellow human beings or kill innocent people. There are, however, exceptions, when you are forced to defend yourself, your family and your nation due to an unavoidable aggression.

Not to forget God even for a moment.

By giving a clear example of a crucial part of physical body, God has emphasized that we should take His presence seriously and not forget Him. If someone is always with somebody to guard him like a secret service agent, could that person forget his own guard! If we cannot see God with our physical eyes that does not mean that He is not present.

We can carry on our jobs, businesses, and other functions of life; at the same time, we should remember Him. God is still close even if we ignore Him just like God's creation oxygen is so close to us whether we acknowledge its presence or not.

Become positively Creative and avoid Destructive actions

We can grow food, feed the whole world, and eliminate poverty and disease instead of manufacturing weapons of mass destruction. Due to the arms race in the world, we are tempted to be ahead of other nations at any cost. Since everyone is going to leave one day through natural causes, why invest trillions of dollars in developing killing machines. You do not hear about world leaders who were in power about fifty years ago. Many such leaders have gone to the next dimension of life and could be facing serious challenges in giving account of their mistakes which caused deaths of millions of innocent people. In the next world there is no argument as one can see one's own life's video and the person can judge himself in the light of that truth.

Why not practice love and compassion

This world is temporary. Even a hundred years of life passes like a dream just like hundreds of years history presented in a movie finishes in two or three hours. Why not live in love and compassion? Why not use our creative instincts instead of destructive abilities so that this world can become a place of peace, compassion and love. There are exceptions when law and order have to be maintained or a nation has to be defended against an aggression.

Hate and anger can distance us from the presence of God.

We can control our emotions and mold our character by replacing negative habits with the positive ones and strive to develop good character. We should not let hate and anger blind our foresight.

10

I Am So Close, I Listen to You

"And when my servant asks thee concerning Me God, surely I am near; I answer the prayer of the servant when he calls upon Me. So let them also obey My call and believe in Me, that they may be guided in the right way."[42]

Thousands of years ago the map of the world was very different. Millions of things have perished since then. But the blessed Face God was there then as it is here today. His blessed Face will still be here forever with all its glory, majesty and honor.

He is now as He was before. He can express Himself through His creatures or He can choose to communicate with us through any channel of communication or means He finds suitable according to His wish. God is free from change and He is near us and in our hearts. He is in the heavens and everything in the universe is surrounded by Him.

We are like machines that have been manufactured by God according to His vision, plan, strategy and wisdom without any suggestions or participation from anybody. He has given us manuals of operation such as His holy books. We must obey and accept God's call and instructions. He responds to His servant's call. You can develop a friendship with Him.

God Responds to Calls

He removes suffering and restores your comforts.

"And when some hurt touches man, he cries to his Lord, turning to Him in repentance. But when He bestows a favor upon him from Himself, he forgets that for which he had cried for before."[43]

The Face of the Friend

Look! The heart is the truth's kernel
The body's the shell

Look! The Face of the Friend
Adorns the robe of the soul

Each atom displays a trace
Of His Being

Look! Is the sunbeam His Light?
Or is it He Himself?

Shah Nimatallah Wali

Call not anyone except God; everything will perish save His Face.

"And call not any other god besides God: There is no god but He. Everything will perish save His Face. To Him belongs the Command, and to Him you (all) shall be brought back.[44]

The only eternal reality is God and the whole phenomenal world is subject to flux and change. He will endure forever while we will pass to the next dimension before His sight.

He is the one who responds to all the needs of His servants.

He furnished all our needs and wants. He knows the needs of His creations before they realize them, and gives them satisfaction even before it is needed. When we are facing a calamity, we call upon Him and He answers our call and rescues us.

I am an ordinary person; but amazingly, whenever I had a question to or a prayer; I received the answer through a dream, a vision, and an inspiration, through the verses and in so many different ways. I have had thousands of personal spiritual experiences which have confirmed my belief of Him being present everywhere. There has never been a situation where I was left without an answer. This shows that He has an infinite ability to listen, see and respond.

I have been shown many major international incidents or events in advance in dreams. I felt as if somebody is always with me guiding and taking care of me. I can hardly find any aspect of my life about which I have not been advised in advance. This is not my ability but God's generosity and forgiveness that He has let me experience His closeness. I have found God extremely loving and caring. So can you.

Whole World Is the Living Mirror of God ('s Attributes)

Seeing with intimacy
If you dwell with the Friend
In genuine intimacy
Then, in the whole world

You will see
The incomparable God
Since the whole World

Is the Living Mirror of God (His attributes)?
It is impossible to see anything
Aside from God.

Sad al Din Hamawi

11

God created Everything from Water

"God has created every moving creature from the water."

Of them there are some that creep on their bellies, and some that walk on two legs, and some that walk on four. God creates what He wills. Verily God is able to do all things. [45]

First everything was water. God created everything from the water. Then He created clay, air, and fire. He created the sun and moon and everything for the service and use of human beings. Our bodies still need more water daily to avoid dehydration because we are seventy percent or more water.

He created us from the water and clay, so that we do not become arrogant and proud but remain aware of our origin. Water is so soft and flexible that it forms the shape of whatever container you pour it into. Pour it into a glass, a jug or a bucket and it takes that shape.

All creations need water for their survival. God has placed water on the earth in many different forms such as saltwater in the oceans, fresh water in the lakes and rivers, frozen water in the form of snow, the mountains, and water in the vegetation.

God created human beings for Himself and the universe for us

You can see everything in creation depends on its Creator. Everything is aware of the presence of God. Everything remembers Him. The birds, animals, mammals, and all vegetation glorify God because their inner selves and outer selves are all in harmony. They always glorify and praise their Creator, God.

Live before God like water not like fire.

Live before God like a flower not like a thorn.

Live like you are in paradise.

All human beings are members of One Body

All human beings
Are the members
Of one body
Every person is a glint
Shining from a single gem

When the world causes pain for one member
How could the other members
Ever rest in peace

If you lack grief
For another one's sorrow
Why call yourself
A human being?

Abu Said Ibn Abi'l Khayr

The volume of Water always remains same in the world.

Imam Ghazzali, a great thinker and a spiritual scholar who lived nine centuries ago, wrote in a book that the total volume of water always remains the same in the world. The water might be in different forms as water in the oceans, rivers, lakes, in the form of snow on the mountains or rain and clouds. The water gets recycled in different forms but retains its balance at all times. The great scholar discovered this secret through his research and spiritual knowledge.

12

The Life as a Soul before Conception?

You were alive as a soul even before your conception.

We need to discover our own selves, before discovering Mars.

Our life in the world of the souls.

You thought that your life started just when you were conceived and later, after nine months of life in the womb, you were born. That is not the true reality.

God first created souls of all the human beings who will be born in this world from the first man to the last man or woman to live on this earth. All souls were coexisting in the world of the souls.

All those people who have yet to be born are already living in the world of the souls as souls. In the beginning of time, God created all the souls and asked these souls who their Creator Lord was. They all replied, "You, our Lord." He wanted to make sure that they do not forget their true God when later engulfed in the life of this world. Good souls always remember this truth that God is their Lord and Creator. When immigrants become citizens, they have to take oath. When God created our souls, we had to take an oath with Him that He is our Lord before coming to this world so that we do not forget Him. Sometimes people coming from different continents meet and realize they have seen each other or met somewhere before not knowing where! What about the term Soul-mates!

Every human being knows that God created him. He might call Him by different name according to his specific faith or religion, but he realizes there is one great power that created him and everything. Our souls know God.

There was one great spiritual man of God called Bayazid Bustami who used to say that he still remembered his oath when he was asked by God: "Who is his Lord?" He remembered his reply, as a soul,

That God, "You are my Lord." He used to say he can never forget Who his Creator is! He soared spiritually beyond heavens while still living in this world due to his intense love of God.

When people love God intensely, they express unusual statements

When some people love God intensely, they express their feelings and say things that might not sound appropriate to other people. But this condition is due to their close relationship with their Creator. Only when you fall in love, you can truly realize what the extraordinary state of mind is.

I feel His presence everywhere and in all beautiful things

I see the fresh flowers of different colors,
I see the birds happily flying above,
I feel the morning breeze,
I see the blue waves of the ocean,
I see the bright sky covered by clouds and then thunder, lightening and rain pouring heavily,
I see the butterfly flying over plants and flowers,
I see the innocent face of a baby and fresh sweet eyes,
I see the sunset, green trees and lake water,
I say all Praise and Glory be to God.
I see the night approaching and the sky above covering with glittering stars and moon shining above, I say Glory and all Praise be to God.

Whatever I see and witness around me, I see His hand and His Presence everywhere and within me.

Expression of Intense Love and Passion for God

The intense love of God intoxicated Mansur Hallaj and he forgot his own self, who he was, due to feeling the overwhelming presence of God. He hardly slept or ate and was dying to meet his Beloved in real. Finally, he got his wish.

I am Love, I am Beloved

I am love, I am beloved; no less am I the lover,
I am the mirror and I am the Beauty,
Therefore behold me in myself.

I am He whom I love, and He whom I love is I:
We are two spirits dwelling in one body,
If thou seest me, thou see Him,
And if thou see Him, thou see us both.

Mansur Al Hallaj

(this poem expresses state of being intoxicated in the Love of
God and being unaware of one's own self)

13

Remember You Were Once a Cell

You the unknown and insignificant

"So Blessed is God, the Best of the Creators." [46]

Now you argue that there is no God and that the world came into being by itself. There was a time when you were simply a cell—an unknown, insignificant, and unimportant cell in the womb of your mother. Who wanted to discuss about an invisible cell? No one even knew you existed. No one wanted to recognize your existence even if you talked about it. You were not even mentionable. Your mother was the first to feel you a few weeks later.

God reminds us human beings:

"There was a time when you were nothing (not mentionable)."

How does man come into this world from a tiny cell?

God creates human beings in stages:

First God created you as a soul. Then, you were as a cell. Then it is a clot of blood. Next it is a piece of flesh. Then a piece of flesh containing blood and bones. Then it is the creation of a human body. Next it is an infant, then a child, a boy or a girl, a teenager, and then an adult. Then the person becomes middle aged, a senior, and at the end of his life becomes childlike again, losing memory, weak and dependent on others. Then he needs others' care to survive just like when he was an infant.

"And indeed We created man out of an extract of clay (water and earth). Thereafter We made him as cells in a safe lodging (womb of the mother). Then We made the cells into a clot (a piece of thick coagulated blood), then We made the clot into a little lump of flesh, then we made out of that little lump of flesh bones, then We clothed the bones with flesh, and then We brought it forth as another creation. So Blessed is

Each Breath Gives Your Soul Life

With knowledge each breath
Will give your soul life.

In ignorance
Each breath
Chips your essence away.

Mahaqqiq Aradabili Bidguli

God, the Best of Creators."[47]

There is so much wisdom in this creative process. This is hard to believe but the wise people remember how they were created, so they can remember their Creator at every stage of their lives. One could question:

Who nourished me when I was a cell?

Who looked after me when I was a cell?
Who protected me from hot and cold when I was a clot of blood?
Who allowed my growth when I became a piece of flesh?
Who ensured my growth in the womb and outside as an infant, boy, teenager, adult, and finally in an old age?
Who created this entire cycle and systems of lives in the universe?
The answer to each of these statements is God, the loving Creator.

Life in the Mother's Womb

Our Mothers: most loving creature of God

Father teaches you how to climb the mountain of life

When our parents got married, through the human productive process, our mothers conceived us, and we were planted in their wombs. According to God's decree, after one hundred and twenty days in the womb, an angel blows the baby's soul in the form of a light into the body. Now the baby starts moving. The heart of the baby starts pumping after the soul enters the baby's body.

The baby grows and is sustained there until reaching the period of nine months, which is a long life for the baby.

The baby does not want to leave the comfort of the womb, where he gets fed automatically and does not have to work to find food. The child screams in protest and pain at leaving that comfortable place when forced out by the doctors and nurses at the time of his birth into this world. That is the pain of leaving the comfortable life in the womb.

Then comes a time later in life, when we have to leave this world for the next world.

> *"He lives in this world like a traveler who stopped at a station to rest and then moves on to the hereafter continuing his life journey..."*[48]

> *"You sow the seeds in the life of the world (your deeds and character in this world) and you will reap the fruits in the next world..."*[49]

A Vision of the Beloved

One night
During prayers
A vision
Of the Beloved
Appeared to me

Lifting the veil
From his Face
He said

Take a good look
At the one
You always leave behind.

14

What Are You Composed of?

Reflect at your own creation!
Do you know what you are made up of?

Who are you? You are composed of five main elements:

water, air, clay, fire and soul.

You are the supreme miracle of God as He has given you the creative process and the ability to rule other creatures in this world. You are supposed to rule the world through guidance from God to ensure perfect justice.

Instead of ruling the world wisely, we are exploiting other creatures like animals in our zoos. We should take care of ourselves and others but we are engaged in killing of our fellow human beings and might reach a level which is lower than even the animals. We are progressing fast toward that level by creating the most powerful weapons that can kill the human race in an instant at the press of a simple button. Our scientists and labs are busy doing research to find ways to vaporize the maximum number of our fellow human beings in the fastest way and shortest possible time and in the cost-effective way.

God's way is not to destroy the world because He is loving, forgiving and patient. We are trying to do that job by creating destructive weapons and pollution. But God loves mankind and wants to save them from self-destruction. When we become close to God, we can live in harmony and peace. All mankind can live like a family.

The Love of God can help us achieve peace without the war

When we are close to God, we can achieve peace and positive results through prayer and negotiation better than what we could do through war. The power of God can help us create superior results peacefully thus preventing the need for war which can destroy both the aggressor and the victim.

O My Purpose and Meaning, Hearing and My Sight

Thy will be done, O my Lord and Master!

Thy will be done, O my purpose and meaning!

O Essence of my being, O goal of my desire,

O my speech and my hints and my gestures!

O all of my all, O my hearing and my sight,

O my whole and my elements and my particles!

Rumi

Each of the five elements mentioned above plays a part in our creation, nature and personality. Our nature is like water, so that we should always remain in surrender and obedience to our Creator.

But the elements of the air take us high; we think we are the greatest, biggest, and tallest—more powerful than the moutains. The mountains feel proud among themselves. The highest mountain feels that it is taller than the other mountains.

But even the mountains are humbled before God.

Some human beings do not even acknowledge that God exists. But the mountains always remain in surrender and humility before their Creator. God says that

Mountains used to join David in glorification and praises of God. [50]

The fire makes us feel arrogant, proud, angry, hateful, violent, and revengeful. The clay makes us want to pile up more possessions, property and wealth in this world.

But the intellect makes us think and act rationally. It inclines us toward spiritual things like faith and wisdom which guide us to treat our neighbors with kindness. It tells us about God who loves us and is compassionate and takes care of us.

God wants us to mold our character and become marvels of His manifestation. We should remember Him and contemplate in his creation and help our fellow human beings in every way we can make a difference in their lives.

The seeker of the blessed Face is always improving himself and character never being satisfied from it until it reaches a point of excellence where he or she can hear God saying in their hearts:

> *"God is pleased with thyself and you be well pleased with God."*[51]

15

God Lets You Live from One Breath to the Next

You do not live by years but by breaths.

We should thank Him for each breath inhaled and exhaled.

God is letting us live from one breath to the next through His presence. He cares for us and protects us from all kinds of harm. How wonderfully He has designed and fashioned our physical body. He did not just create lungs but established a respiratory system in us to perform breathing process even when we are asleep. He programmed our lungs and organs so that they can do their jobs efficiently without our direction. What about the blood circulation? Blood runs through our veins which stretch for miles. Circulation goes on nonstop from the time of our birth to our last breath. Thanks to the Almighty Creator for making everything so perfect and easy for us.

Consider how oxygen is supplied to the brain, how food is digested so the body can absorb the useful elements and discard the waste, how blood is purified, and the intricacies of the nervous system.

Who could create such a perfect mechanism?

One wonders who has taught each organ of our bodies to perform certain functions. Each part of our bodies is programmed to perform functions automatically. We are the greatest miracle to be studied!

Who ensures the creation and recreation of cells in our bodies?

Billions of cells carry out their functions. Blood continues to circulate through our bodies each moment whether we are awake or asleep. Cells die and new cells are created in our bodies each day. God is controlling this for us, yet we are not thankful.

Is there any power, other than God with infinite wisdom, power, and energy? No!

The Beloved gives me life

Love came and I gave up my soul to the Beloved,

The Beloved now gives me life from His own life

Love came and like blood filled my veins and tissues,

Emptied me of myself and filled me with the Friend.

The Friend has taken possession of every Atom of my being.

The name is all that I have left now: all the rest is He.

Rumi

16

The Purpose of Creation

"I was a hidden Treasure, I wished to be known; so I created the human beings." says God. [52]

The purpose and function of the human beings is to know and discover the hidden beloved and represent Him. Once we know Him, we will fall in love and become attached to Him. He inspires us with love, wisdom, knowledge so that we can inspire our fellow human beings to get closer to Him. He is the source of love which He has poured in the hearts of our mothers, fathers, brothers, sisters, spouses, sons, daughters, other relations, and all human beings. Hence, He should be the goal of our devotion.

It is worth repeating that God says that He has created everything for us and us for Himself. We have been created to love God, so He can love us too.

"We have created man and jinn for our worship." [53]

He is close to all His creations.

As has been said before, God has total control of the universe and He can stop things and events from happening. Only God can bestow visible and invisible favors, rewards and gifts. No one really has the power to benefit you or cause you loss. Other elements can create illusion of fear and doubt. He is the only One Who merits our focus, worship, adoration, obedience, and service.

All the beautiful creations in the heaven and the earth, harmony, balance, mountains, oceans, seas, sunsets, and flowers are the work of His hand.

The Life's Destiny Is the Vision of God

We can achieve this goal through intense loving and remembering Him constantly. The veils will lift up one by one.

There is nothing more precious in this world and in the next world than the vision of God. We should develop love, passion, thoughts, attachment, and longing for God. If you love Him, God will create love for you in the hearts of people. All creations and angels will love you, too. How great is that!

You are like a Fish asking:
Where's the Water?

In a vision I asked
the Master of Wisdom
Can you explain to me
The Names,
Attributes,
and the Essence?
Of the Lord of Lords?

He replied:
"You're just like a fish
Asking the waves and the bubbles
Can you show me the way to the water?"

Maftun Hamadani

Everything is created with a specific purpose.

Everything in this universe has a specific meaning and purpose. For example, take the honeybee, it makes a thousand trips to the garden flowers, so it can produce the honey for its offspring and for the use of human beings. The silkworm creates the beautiful fiber for the use of human beings. The fibers of the silkworm's cocoon are treated, spun, and woven into fabric. There are so many kinds of seafood that have become delicacies enjoyed by mankind. There are so many plants and herbs used to produce medicine.

17

God is Watching Everything

He is watchful of all His creation

"For God sees well all that they do."[54]

God watches all human beings living on this earth with compassion and loving care. He is aware of our intentions, thoughts and actions all the time. He is watching all activities that can disturb the divine harmony and balance in the universe. All our actions are preserved in an invisible record or a chip.

Are you aware that God is watching you and everything? If you are aware of this reality, you should become careful not to cross the divine limits and laws just as you are careful not to break the country's traffic and other laws.

His presence is everywhere in the heavens and on earth.

His presence is in the cities, in the countryside, and on the mountains—wherever you might be. He bears patiently with people until they realize and turn to the positive way.

God is the ultimate witness to everything.

Nothing in the universe can escape the observation of God.

God is present everywhere and observes all things and is thus a witness to all actions and events at all times. We cannot hide anything because our lives are like an open book before God. We now have video cameras which enable us to see what is happening thousands of miles away. God is able to see and provide for even a small insect inside a mountain

Watchfulness is like a law enforcement action when our activities are watched in case we break and lose respect for the laws. When you observe someone doing something wrong, you are a witness to that action and may be called to court to give testimony regarding what you witnessed.

Of the Friend's Face

The Rust
Of strangers
Any heart who resides
In the Beloved's alley
Becomes a confidant
Of the Court of Secrets

File away
The rust of strangers
From the heart's mirror
Then it will deserve
The splendor
Of the Friend's Face.

Gulzar Isfahani

Becoming conscious of the fact that God is watching us

You and I can become close to God just as He is so close to us by becoming conscious of the fact that He is witnessing all our actions, affairs, movements, plans, good virtues and injustices. This consciousness can help improve our thoughts, character, and daily dealings.

The Prophet Muhammad said that **"the deen (religion) is dealings."**

People need to be conscious of God when they are dealing with any other human being, relatives or others. A person's faith, worship and relationship with God should be reflected in his behavior with other people.

18

God is Beyond Time, Space, and Material

No past or future, it is always now

For God, one day is equal to our one thousand years. For Him there is no past or future because He is beyond the limits of time. He cannot be limited to a specific place. He says that He is everywhere. For Him, the earth is but a tiny speck in space.

He is beyond distance measurement, space and time, days and nights, dimensions, directions, weight and form. He is beyond the seven heavens, all celestial bodies, and all things. Everything far and near is close to Him. The directions east, west, south, and north have no significance to Him.

When you switch to frequency of closeness to God, you too can experience no time and space.

He is infinite and beyond all material limits. There is no space or place that is hidden from His presence. When you watch a specific television channel, you are focused on that channel while hundreds of other channels are functioning at the same time. But you know and feel what is happening in that channel before your eyes. Similarly, when you are meditating and seeking the pleasure and closeness of God, there are times when you too can spiritually experience the state of no time and space. Nothing is impossible before God.

One day equals thousand years of our reckoning

"He manages and regulates every command or affair (Action) from the heavens to the earth; then it (affair) will go up to Him, in one Day, the span whereof is a thousand years of your reckoning (our time count)."[55]

I gazed into my heart; there I saw Him,

He was nowhere else
Cross and Christians, from end to end,
I surveyed; He was not on the cross.
I went to the idol-temple, to the ancient pagoda;
No trace was visible there.
I went to the mountains of Herat and Kandahar
I looked; He was not in that hill or dale,
With set purpose I fared to the summit of Mount Qaf
In that place was only Angel's habitation
I bent the reins of search to the Ka'aba (Mecca),
He was not in that resort of old and young
I questioned Ibn Sina of His state;
He was not within Ibn Sina's range,
I fared towards the scene of two bow-lengths distance,
He was not in that exalted court,
I gazed into my heart;
There I saw Him; He was nowhere else.

Rumi

All the decrees and events that are going to happen in the world come from God to the earth in one day, which is equivalent to one thousand years of our time. It is possible to presume that the decisions, decrees, and affairs that are supposed to take place one thousand years from now according to our reckoning have already been issued.

One should develop closeness to God in order to experience timelessness. When you contemplate and worship God with true love, you lose sight of time and space. In true spiritual dreams, you can travel to the heavens and the earth and experience many years of journey in a matter of few minutes or hours.

19

God is the Most Generous and Bountiful

His treasures are like the oceans.

"O man, what has made you careless concerning your Generous and Bountiful Lord? Who created you, and then fashioned and made you complete, and then made you in the best of forms. He is infinitely Generous (the Source of all Generosity)."[56]

When God bestows on you the gifts of wealth and fame, it becomes a challenge as to how you use these gifts. It should be without arrogance and pride. You should be able to fully appreciate God's generosity, knowing that none of what is given to us is ours forever but is given to us in trust.

God says that if all the humanity that ever existed from the beginning of the world to the end were to stand before Him and ask for wealth as much as the richest person on this earth has, God the most generous would provide wealth to all the people more than their requests and this distribution of wealth would not even be like a drop in the oceans.

God's greatest generosity is His love and mercy. He helps you even before you ask.

He is generous beyond your imagination and His treasures are like the oceans that never run dry. His greatest generosity is His mercy, through which He forgives and wipes out sins when He could punish. His generosity and rewards surpass all expectations. He is always generous in forgiving the sins of people unless they have done something so serious as to take some innocent person's life. In that case, the person has to satisfy the claims of the victim before God can forgive him because he was unjust. He is so generous that He will find excuses to forgive and reward people beyond their expectations. He gives us warnings of punishment, so that we do not engage in oppression against our fellow human beings.

Your Heart Is a Mirror

Since your heart is a mirror
Take a look there.

Even a wise eye
Your names reflect
Your boundless Essence

The world displays
Your living signs

The stars trace out
You're very proof

If not enraptured
By your charms, well
Even a wise eye
Is truly blind

Maftun Hamadani

The Source of all Prosperity

God can enrich you with abundance.

God is infinitely rich, self-sufficient and has no needs. His treasures are beyond measure. His treasures always remain full even after distribution of riches to the whole world. It's like taking a bucket full of water from the ocean which makes no difference in the level of water in the oceans.

He creates abundance in peoples' lives each moment. He gives them wealth so that they can enjoy and become distributors to other human beings. But most people disregard the needs of others and think all the wealth and riches they have accumulated are due to their hard work. They can plant seeds of generosity which continues growing forever.

If they were to distribute their wealth to their fellow human beings wisely through work and projects, their riches would multiply beyond their imagination. But they are not aware of this.

God invites all human beings to engage in trading and business which consists of charitable projects. It will never have a loss and will grow forever producing dividends in this world as well as in the next.

The Burning and Melting

Learning to Burn
The day love's fire was lit,
The lover learnt
The way of burning
From the Beloved

This burning and melting
Is the Friend's doing

If the candle were never lit,
The moth would never burn.

Abu Said Abi al-Khayr

20

God's Infinite Patience

His presence and patience are ignored by most.

He is infinitely patient. Patience is a divine quality. God loves and rewards those who exercise patience and are persevering. If you have this quality, you will refuse things of haste that your flesh and ego desire. People experience difficulties in their lives due to lack of patience. Millions of marriages break up because partners, who used to love each other, become impatient with each other's behavior and can no longer take it. Through patience, they can grow their ties stronger.

"Paradise is surrounded by things that the flesh does not want."[57]

In the face of difficulties, your self and body might suffer, but you should remain steadfast. This is a quality highly appreciated by God and He can inspire solutions to positively resolve difficult situations.

Many among us deny and disobey Him, oppress His good servants and other human beings. God is all-knowing and patiently watches all these injustices. He waits until a certain time when he takes account of the oppressors.

"He is with those who are patient." [58]

He is patient in His actions and His dealings with His creation. He knows those breaking His laws and commandments, but He gives them time to realize their mistakes and turn to Him in repentance. Like the criminals in the prisons are fed, sheltered, and protected by the government, God is more compassionate. He, too, knows the arrogant, oppressors, and those who deny His existence, but He sends them their sustenance and protects them from harm. He has set an appointed time for everything and when this point reaches, then there is no turning back. The great Prophet Moses continuously warned Pharaoh not to be arrogant and oppress his people but Pharaoh ignored his warnings. Then when that decisive point came, Pharaoh and his army were drowned leaving no trace of them. This story is related in the three great scriptures Torah, Bible and Quran.

Patience is a very noble virtue for the believer. No success or perfection can be achieved easily and without pain. Only the truly patient reap rewards for going through suffering, misfortunes, poverty, accident, and sickness. We need to become aware of God's presence and surrender our desires and passions to Him. Sometimes we are tested.

"If God touches you with affliction, there is none that can relieve you from that except Him, and if He touches you with good fortune there is none that can stop it for He is able to do all things."[59]

"Patience has been mentioned ninety places in the Quran!" [60]

An affliction caused by a friend is a gift, and it is a sin to wail after receiving it. Patience endears us to Almighty God.

God loves those who are firm and steadfast. Those who cultivate the habit of patience are beloved to God. How can man suffer indignity with whom God takes sides? When God is on his side, no harm can come to him. Patience alone makes one the leader, and he is entrusted with the duty of guiding people.

"And we appointed from among them, leaders, giving guidance under Our command, when they achieved firm faith and persevered with patience."[61]

The patience of a person serves as a weapon of defense against the wiles and cunning of his foes. If you remain constant and do right, it is certain you will overcome them ultimately. So persevere patiently.

The Moon of Your Love

Not a single soul lacks
A pathway to you

There's no stone
No flower
Not a single piece of straw
Lacking your existence

In every particle of the world
The moon of your Love
Causes the heart
Of each atom to glow.

Muhammad Shirin Maghribi

Just as the affectionate father and mother take care of their children, more so also God takes care of His creatures during tribulation. The essence of patience lies in concealing tribulation. As long as the person keeps complaining about his problems to others, the difficulties linger longer.

"I only complain of my distraction and anguish to God."[62]

What the King does is a thing of beauty. Mentally, mankind should acknowledge that the Ruler of the universe knows the art of running the universe and its affairs. All His actions are based on perfect wisdom.

21

God is Seeing Everything in the Universe

Our past, present and future is like an open book in His sight

"No vision can grasp Him, but He grasps all vision. He is the Most Subtle and Well-Aware of all things."[63]

The entire universe and all creatures in it are before the sight of God Who has bestowed on us the ability of seeing from His own power of seeing? You have eyes, but you are not the owner of the sight that is outside of you. Eyes are instruments to capture sight. We have the respiratory system within us and the oxygen we breathe is outside of us. Our eyes are like the electric bulb, but the bulb would not illuminate unless connected to electrical current. God enables our eyes to connect to the sight so we can clearly see. Many people have eyes but they cannot see as they are not connected to the sight.

The past, present, and future is before Him

He sees all His creatures even those hidden at the bottom of mountains and oceans. He sees all that has passed, all there is, and all there will be until the end of time. God has given mankind and most of His other creations the ability to see. Some of His creatures see shapes, colors, and movement better than men do. Some creations (e.g., snakes) have sensors through which they can sense the presence of objects. God can enable one to see even if one doesn't have eyesight.

God is the best scientist and He created the science.

Eyes are a wonderful miracle of God, but only the blind truly appreciate the value of eyes. The eye sight is one of God's many gifts. As we get older our eyes become weaker. The ability to see is loaned to us by God. If the ability to see was our own, we would never relinquish it at any age. In older age, we gradually surrender our eyesight to God, its original owner, and finally in an advanced age, we are unable to see, and we need the support of eye glasses and other people to guide us.

The Essence is One, but the Attributes many.

Remember the Truth
The soul is love and affection
So know the soul

But the Truth is ecstasy, forgetting your self.
When "I" and "you" are present
You're thinking from

The Ego's place
If you hear those two words,
Then remember the Truth.

Saghir Isfahani

Angels to protect and guard every human being until certain time

He is seeing not only what is on the outside of us, but what is in our hearts. He knows our intentions, goals, and plans. God has appointed angels to protect and guard every human being. Our entire life story is captured by these angels in a spiritual chip.

How would it be if we were to see the movie of our own life?

How would we feel when we see the video of our own lives displaying injuries and injustices we have caused to our fellow human beings? When the person will see the work of his own hands, he will not be able to argue as he will see everything he has done. This is incredible spiritual technology because in that dimension only truth can exist and the action are compared with that truth. There is absolutely nothing negative in the kingdom of God; it is all light. The falsehood is darkness and it cannot exist in the light.

We should exercise control over our tongues

"There is a guard (angel) assigned on the right and one on the left of every person. Every word expressed by each person is recorded by these angels."[64]

The angel on the right captures the good words and actions and the angel on the left captures negative words and actions. When the man will see this DVD he will be shocked to notice the perfection of the record as not even the smallest thing could escape the record. So we should take care of what we say.

God uses all these techniques to motivate human beings to achieve perfection in their characters and lives through self-improvement.

Every Moment is more precious than the diamonds

The seeker becomes conscious of the reality of life and finds it very difficult to disobey His commands, rules, and regulations. The seeker who loves God will cry to see the moments he wasted in his life. Every moment is more precious than the diamonds which have no usefulness in the sight of God except to provide temporary beauty, luxury and consolation to those who wear them.

22

God Hears Everything

"My God knows (every) word (spoken) in the heavens and on earth. He is the One who hears and knows all things."[65]

In order to fulfill the needs of all creation, at all times, to monitor and control every action, every movement in the universe one has to be able to hear every appeal, every request, and every need. God has the infinite power of hearing everything at all times. That means He hears every sound, every whisper, every secret, and every voice. If one wonders how is it possible? Just look at the man's innovative brain power.

God has created the human brain as a super computer

A super computer can perform billions of transactions per second. What about God who bestowed the gift of brain to human beings to invent so powerful computers. Where can you find a better super computer than the brain? The most powerful thinking machine has helped achieve many scientific discoveries and technological advancement in the world.

If you talk to Him, you will get the answer.

He hears what is spoken and what remains as thoughts in our minds. He hears all the languages of His creations like the ants, insects, birds, and animals. No obstacle can come between the communication of God and His creation. You can try to talk to Him and you will get the answer.

You can communicate with your Creator twenty-four/seven.

You can communicate directly with your loving creator at any time and anywhere. You do not need the help of an attorney or third party to talk to God. It is only you and Him. You can share all your concerns, anxieties, and secrets with the most generous and caring Friend. No power and government can tap or hinder the communication between you and God. He hears and responds in a timely way to the call of every person, especially those who have been oppressed and wronged.

For those who love God, He becomes their eyes, ears, hands and feet as is stated in the Qudsi traditions:

> *"My servant comes close to Me with his continuous devotion until I love him and when I love him I become his ears with which he hears and his eyes with which he sees and his hands with which he works or strikes and feet with which he walks."* [66]

23

"I am God, the One True Lord."

"Verily I am God, the Lord of all Creations."67

"O' Moses, I am God. Indeed, there is no god except Me. So worship Me and establish prayer for My Remembrance."68

His blessed Face is everywhere before our sight. Where can one run away from His presence and kingdom? He knows our lives better than we know ourselves. Nothing is invisible to Him, and every secret is clearly known to Him like an open book. He knows every beat of our hearts.

God tells the earth to produce his ashes.

A man sinned greatly against himself, and when death came to him he told his sons, saying: When I have passed away, burn me and scatter my ashes into the sea, for, by God if my Lord takes possession of me, He will punish me in a manner in which He has punished no one else. So they carried out his wishes after he passed away.

> *Then God said to the earth: Produce every particle of his ashes and bring him before Me what you have taken — and there he was! And God said to him: What induced you to do what you did? The man replied: I did not see anything good in my life's actions. Being afraid of You! O my Lord because of that God forgave him. So do not think one can escape from God but remember that He is forgiving and merciful.* [69]

Reflect and examine the wonderful creations of the heavens and the earth, and you will realize that without a great designer this workmanship is not possible. The human soul naturally testifies that God exists and that everything is governed by His laws. For this reason God says:

"Is there any doubt about God, the Creator of heavens and earth?"

Turning Your Soul to the Eternal Sun

When traveling
Love's pathway,
Never stop
Turning your soul

Toward the eternal sun.
But since the Real
Shines forth

From every direction,
Why aim your prayers
At only one spot?

Fayd Fayyadi

24

God Knows and is Aware of Everything

"And God hears and Knows all things."[71]

"We created man and We know what thoughts go through his mind."[72]

God is the source of all knowledge, and His knowledge is infinite. He has the knowledge of visible and invisible. He knows what has happened, what is happening, and what will happen from the beginning to the end. All existence is present at all times in the knowledge of God.

Our knowledge stays on the surface of a very few things. We do not know what is going to happen to us in the next moment. We think we do, but anything can happen in an instant. What is this human life in comparison to the infinite life?

He has given us freedom, we do whatever we like.

Indeed God bestows on us countless blessings. He has given us freedom, we do whatever we like. He taught us what is right and what is wrong. We should strive to know God and seek His pleasure. Eternal salvation is contained within all that.

God can bestow wisdom on you through the purity and love with which He created you. It will be yours without instruction, study or learning. We should strive to know God and His attributes so that we will start feeling His presence and His beauty, generosity and love all the time.

Not a leaf falls without His knowledge.

"And with Him are the Keys of the unseen. None knows them but He. And He knows whatever there is in the land and in the sea; not a leaf falls, but He Knows it and there is not a grain in the darkness of the earth nor anything fresh or dry, but is written in a clear record."[73]

Friendship with God

When the morning of friendship
with God begins to dawn,

the soul becomes distant
from the entire world

You then reach a place in which
each breath of the soul,

Without the eye's hindrance,
Can see the Friend.

Sayf al Din Bakharzi

Nothing in the universe is hidden from God. He is fully aware of everything hidden and manifest. He is the One Who is aware of the hidden inner actions and movement of everything. He is the One Who can reach the deepest, darkest, hidden corners of His kingdom, where neither human intelligence nor His angels can penetrate. None can escape His awareness and knowledge

One should know that there is nothing that we do in secret, or think of doing, that is not in the knowledge of God. We should cultivate good intentions, goodwill and wish all humanity peace, harmony and healing. Good thoughts and intentions are rewarded with unexpectedly positive results.

25

God Is the Most Compassionate and Gracious

"In the Name of God, the Most Gracious, the Most Merciful."[74]

"Say: Call upon God or call upon the Most Compassionate."[75]

This universe is functioning because of the infinite grace and compassion of God. He is sustaining and cherishing all living creatures through His mercy, without any distinction between the believer and disbeliever.

He created us and everything out of His infinite love. God is beneficent. We too should apply the attribute of compassion in our lives by caring for those in distress. We should demonstrate compassion by helping to alleviate the pain and suffering of others.

"Who is the One who removes your distress and suffering?" [76]

All other creations, when presented with the option of freedom of choice, remained in surrender and refused to have freedom of choice, but man opted for freedom of choice. Because of our choices, we go through much hardship in our lives, except those who are fortunate and enriched by God. They should be willing to assist those in pain, and those in unfortunate circumstances with grace, compassion, and pity. When you help to remove the suffering of your fellow human beings, you are showing the compassion that God has bestowed on you.

God is ready to accept us with the wings of mercy, love, and pity when we turn to Him with sincerity. Each human being takes his share of the mercy from the merciful God in accordance with his potential.

Your Glance

The heart's love
With your beautiful
intoxicated glance

You are the candle
The entire world is your fluttering moth.

Our souls, our hearts
You made them crazy with love,

You quickly became the home of our hearts
And our hearts, now, are also your home.

Qasim Anwar

26

God's Infinite Mercy

My Mercy prevails and supersedes my wrath.

"God has created mankind in the form of His Mercy."[77]

He is the source of infinite mercy and beneficence. He rewards His obedient servants with eternal gifts and bounties. His Mercy encompasses everything.

> *"Never despair from the mercy of your Lord. He can forgive all sins. He is the most Forgiving and most Merciful."* [78]

He advises us never to despair from God's infinite mercy. We can always find Him full of compassion and mercy regardless of the magnitude of our wrongs.

> *"If your sins are as much as the oceans, My mercy (forgiveness) is bigger than the oceans."*[79]

We should never despair of His mercy and always expect best from Him. Every person is in need of mercy, forgiveness, patience, and grace from the most merciful God. Even though we disobey Him, He is always protecting and preserving us from calamities and guiding us in all aspects of our lives. We should be thankful and always try to seek the pleasure of God by doing great works.

The manifestation of mercy in the believers happens when we help relieve the pain and suffering of others. We feel restless to see others in difficulties and we feel compelled to help them. It is a clear demonstration of the virtues of mercy and compassion that God has implanted in us. Let's acknowledge these attributes by reaching out to those who need assistance and guidance.

Single Breath

It's only one breath
From disbelief's world
To the place
Where faith resides

It's only one sigh
From doubt's way station
To the homeland of certainty

Don't now despise
This single dear breath
The Purpose of Life
Is just this Breath.

Shah Nimatallah Wali

27

God Is the Creator of Everything

He is the source of all life.

"That is God, your Lord! There is no deity but Him, the Creator of all things." [80]

He is the one who creates everything from nothing. He has created both visible and invisible worlds. God is the creator of the heavens and the earth, night and day, life and death, and the life in the hereafter.

He is creating new creations every moment.

He establishes how, when, and where creation will take place. Everything from the beginning to the end of the created existence has been established in wisdom. In accordance with the perfect order, everything follows a specific system and a program. There are no surprises and accidents in the universe.

We are born with dual personality—an outer and inner self. We have the external parts of the body, but there are more elements within us than there are in the outer self. Our desires, passions, habits, thoughts, intentions, ambition, intuition, spirituality, selves, souls or spirits, feelings, emotions are within us.

God has created you as His best creation.

God created the universe with a purpose and infinite love for the creations. His best creation, the human beings are supposed to love Him and seek the presence of the blessed Face of God who is everywhere all the time because of his majesty and power.

The human beings should discover His beauty and perfection.

Just to reiterate, God says: "I was a hidden treasure. Then I wanted to make Myself Known, so I created creation." Our responsibility is to strive for Him and discover the hidden beauty and perfection of His treasure.

Religion Is Nothing Except Your Love

Religion is nothing
Except your love

Awareness is nothing
Except your thought

Should the world being
On a thousand pains

I've lost the knowledge
Of your Love.

Sayyid Hasan Ghaznawi

All creation, and the order that it follows, is beneficence and wisdom. One must discover these qualities and use them for his own benefits and for others. This magnificent creation is nothing but a reflection of the Creator's attributes of beauty, power and energy.

Your inner self cannot lie; it follows only truth. Your outer self follows images, shadows, pictures, and false objects. Your outer self might deny the presence of God, but your inner self knows the presence of God. Your self knows the true one God and Lord. Get to know your inner self in order to know God.

Who created oxygen for our free use and survival?

Nothing in the universe can survive without the life support from God. **Oxygen is always all around us; we don't have to carry it with us. He created the oxygen everywhere in this world for our use and survival.**

When He created the first human being. He thought, planned, and designed the human beings. All these functions took place in one instant. Through His wisdom, He created the plants, trees, and forests to produce oxygen.

Can you live without the oxygen for a few moments?

He is supplying to all those who need oxygen every moment without any assistance from any government, institution, agency, or other power. God is allowing you to continue breathing from one moment to another without your asking for it. This shows His wisdom.

He has created oxygen everywhere in every region of the globe so that we can live and move on to any regions of the earth. He has made oxygen free of any cost, and we can get it effortlessly and without any limit. This shows His generosity.

For a moment, imagine that some government or country controlled the supply of oxygen. It could provide this crucial element of survival only to loyal groups of people and deny its enemies of oxygen. Mankind would be in jeapordy. God is so gracious that He provides oxygen to both those who obey Him and those who don't obey Him. He is so gracious.

I Am wherever You Turn

If He is in sight wherever you look,
Why cast a blind eye
When it comes to you?

The Real said to you
I'm wherever you turn-

So why don't you take
A closer look at yourself?

Dard Shiku

Many people call everything science. Then one can ask:

Who created the gravity? Who created the Mother Nature? Who created the brain that thinks? Who created science? Everything is the creation of God! Is it possible for millions of planets to float in the space in perfect harmony and without ever colliding because of God's design? We can raise millions of such questions and the answer to each will be - God.

God Almighty created the universe with all its planets spinning in space for billions of years without any collision. On the other hand, we human beings fall into conflict with our fellow human beings for even a few yards of land, especially if it happens to be at the border of two countries.

Mother Nature is actually the Hand of God

When people see hurricanes, storms, drought, floods, snow-storms, they call these events as the work of Mother Nature. In fact, it is the Hand of God. Mother Nature is a term to hide the reality and name of the real Doer - God Almighty. He is ninety-nine times more loving to human beings than a mother to her child. So mother nature is actually the Hand of God and His love for us.

Should the Sun change its course, which will be end of the world

If the sun were to come a few miles closer to earth, we could perish. But God would not allow the sun to disobey His command. So the sun is obedient to its Creator. The sun is going through its life cycle as envisioned by God. It doesn't matter if you are religious or not. You have to acknowledge the Creator of actions as He is the source of all creation and recreation everywhere. We could learn from the pattern of obedience to God by each element in the universe. The entire universe is in surrender to its Creator, God.

28

God is Surrounding all Creations

His irresistible power, compassion, knowledge, wisdom, subtle care, and love envelope everything.

The worlds, the heavens, and everything in them are in total surrender willingly or unwillingly to God, except mankind. We are too arrogant and proud to surrender to the One who is so close to us and is the eternal owner of everything.

God has surrounded all His creation from without and within with His irresistible power. The worlds and the heavens bow before Him. How many leaders, empires, civilizations, races, and nations were destroyed when their oppression, arrogance, and rebellion went beyond all boundaries of decency and the mercy and compassion of God? Just like all governments in this world have laws, rules, regulations, and justice to maintain peace and order, God also has laws. A police officer sees a crime, it is investigated and the criminal is sent to prison. When somebody secretly commits a crime against an innocent person, God has implanted the sense of right and wrong which sometimes keep the aggressor restless until the wrong is corrected.

God has overwhelming love for all His creations, but He has also created causes and means that separate His punishing destructive force from His delicate loving finesse. He has created the means of faith, sincerity, justice, compassion, generosity, wisdom, and other beautiful characteristics manifesting His love. He has created the causes of rebellion, denial, arrogance, ignorance, tyranny, and hypocrisy on which the darkness of His wrath is manifested. We are in refuge from God's anger toward God's infinite mercy.

This Universe is perhaps yet Incomplete
I hear the sounds of "Be, and "It is."

I may convey the secret of divine if I have Gabriel's breath
What can these stars tell me of my fate
They are lost themselves in the boundless firmament
The total absorption of thought and vision is life
Scattered thought is selfhood's total death
Pleasures of selfhood are blessings of God
Who makes me lose my awareness of myself
With a pure heart, a noble aim, a poignant soul
The Prophet's 'Mairaj' (ascension) has taught me that
Heaven lies within the bounds of human reach
This universe, perhaps, is yet incomplete
For I hear repeated sounds of, "Be, and "It is."

Sir Dr. Mohammad Iqbal,
The Poet of the East

29

All Creations Glorify God

God is the most praiseworthy

"See you not that to God prostrate in worship all things that are in the heavens and on earth. The sun, the moon, the stars, the hills, the trees, the animals and a great number among mankind? But a great number are (rebellious) such as are fit for punishment"...[81]

"See you not that GodWhose praises all beings in the heavens and on earth do celebrate, and the birds with wings outspread? Each one knows its own (mode of) prayer and praise. And God knows well all that they do."[82]

All the creations glorify God in their own specific languages and sounds. These creatures know who their Creator is. So they acknowledge and appreciate His care and presence. But only some human beings know and praise their Creator.

All praises, merits, virtues originate from Him. He deserves our total devotion. We must praise, glorify, and love God. We must thank, remember, adore, honor, and worship Him with sincerity and purity of our hearts

God is the final goal for us to meet Him one day.

"To God is the final Goal." [83]

God initiates your life and brings the life cycle to an end. Everyone returns to their Originator and Creator. You wonder where all the great civilizations of the past history have gone. Where are the great kings, the great heroes, generals, and the presidents of the great nations? What a wonderful statement expressed by the famous poet that this world is a stage and every human being plays his or her role here.

After playing their roles in this world, the great heroes, writers, artists, thinkers, scientists, generals and leaders have gone to the next phase of life in the hereafter. They and others will reap the fruits of their deeds, good or bad, in the next world. Wise people start saving for their retirement from the early years. Likewise, we should do great works to reap the fruits in the next world.

> *"Now no person knows what delights of the eyes are kept hidden (in reserve as a reward) for their good deeds."* [84]

We are fortunate as we still have the gift of life to revolutionize our lives positively forever.

We are fortunate to still have the gift of life. We still have the opportunity to make a difference in peoples' lives. We can change the course of our lives by becoming more loving, compassionate, patient and serving. We should aim to get closer to God each day and strive to create a spiritual revolution in our lives. The revolution of acquiring great character and noble habits.

Atom Blazed Brighter than a Thousand Suns

Touched by Your Grace
Every soul rejoices
If touched by your grace

Tasting your favor
Is eternal good fortune

When your grace touched an atom
For only a Moment
That atom blazed brighter
Than a thousand Suns.

Majd al din Baghdadi

30

God is Alive and Eternal

He has no similarity to anything in existence.

"God, there is no god but He, the All-Living, the Self-sustaining."[85]

Everything will perish except the blessed Face of God.

God is the living (One): there is no god but Him. You can call on Him with sincere devotion. All Praises are for Him the Lord of the universe. Where is the similarity of the Creator and the created, the fashioner and the fashioned? There is nothing like Him. He existed and controlled his kingdom and the universe when He created it. All actions are His. The value of each life is judged by the extent of the knowledge actions of the person.

God has given lives of different degrees and kinds to His Creation. He has honored man with superior life and intellect, so that man is king over all other creations. Man grows plants, vegetables, flowers, and trees. Man can cultivate crops, rear animals, and fish etc. God has given us the ability to rule the worlds through our intellect and freedom. Men differ also in the degree of their aliveness, which is judged by the extent of their knowledge and their action. You can become alive and aware and conscious of the truly alive One.

God Is Eternal

He has no beginning and no end.

God is the eternal one. Time only exists for the changing creation. There was no time before but God existed. He created the sun, moon, stars, and the space to enable us to keep track of time. He is above and beyond the space and time.

My Only Love Is You

I will pass beyond belief and religion

Because your love is higher

How long can I keep this love a secret?

My only Love is You, beyond rite and ritual.

Ayn al Qudat Hamadani

This world is but a guest house

This world is but a guesthouse where the visitor stays for a while and then leaves to continue his journey. No one is left in this world forever.

Everything in this world and the universe is transitory; the only One who has permanence is God.

Words that emanate from God are eternal along with His attributes. He is without change. His knowledge is eternal. Whatever takes place in His creation is within His knowledge from eternity. His will to make an event at the appointed time has got connection with His eternal knowledge:

> God is Wise by His Knowledge,
> Living with His Life,
> Mighty with His Power,
> Willing with His Will,
> Speaking with His Words and Silence
> Seeing with His Sight,
> Enlightening with His Light
> Hearing with His Hearing

These attributes belong to His eternal attributes. No action or movement can take place without His permission. Every event in the world is His action, creation, and invention.

If one works for God's pleasure and for the benefit of all mankind, he will see the rewards of his hardwork.

Love comes to the protection of these two lost souls.

When you look at His gentleness,

stones and boulders become wax;

when you look at His severity,

even your wax becomes granite.

His mercy comes before His wrath;

if you want spiritual priority, seek the prior attributes.

God is the only object worthy of our love

for He is the true beloved.

Rumi

31

God is Subtle, Gentle and Fine

He is gentle, soft, and at times severe.

"Does he not know Who has created him? He is subtle, cognizant."[86]

He is the most delicate, gentle, beautiful One. He understands the finest mysteries and the details of everything. He has created our bodies in all their complexities and mysteries. God's power to understand intricate details implies an ability to regard things invisible to man. This quality implies as fine and subtle as to be imperceptible to human sight. His purity is so subtle as to be beyond comprehension. God has sight as perfect as to see and understand the finest mysteries, a nature as kind and gracious as to bestow gifts of the most refined kind, and He is extraordinarily gracious and understanding.

God's attributes can be divided into two categories: the attributes of the essence and the attributes of the acts.

The first category of names consist of the attributes of the essence like God is the living, the powerful, and the all-seeing. The second category includes names whose opposites are also God's names, such as the exalter, the abaser, the life giver, and the life taker.

Many of the attributes of the acts can be divided into two further categories that are known as the attributes of gentleness and the attributes of severity.

Emptiness – Only God remains

For someone whose trade is emptiness?
And whose work is annihilation,
The search for certainty, knowledge,

And religion
Has come to an end

Since he's annihilated,
Only God remains
Just God

This is the meaning of
"When poverty becomes complete,
You find God."

Abud Said Abe al Khayr

God says:"My Mercy prevails over My Wrath."[87]

This statement can be interpreted as:

My gentle names take precedence over My severe names.

Wherever you see an act of mercy, you should know that it is from God's presence. The joy and beauty inherent in all of creation and dominating in all of its forms may be said to derive from this way of looking at God's attributes.

All creation is a manifestation of God's severe and gentle names, but the later always take precedence over the former.

Whenever we see the manifestation of wrath and severity, e.g. in suffering and evil, we should know that God's mercy and gentleness will soon manifest themselves. God will soon restore peace, calm, healing and prosperity.

Laughter tells of Thy gentleness, and

lamentation complains of Thy severity.

In the world, these two conflicting messages

tell of a single Beloved.

Rumi

Hidden Away (Your Face)

I haven't seen your rose garden
In a very long time

Nor you're half-intoxicated
Languishing
Narcissus eyes

You've hidden yourself away
From humanity
Like truth

We haven't seen **Your Face**
In a very long time.

Rumi

32

The Lord of Majesty, Honor, and Greatness

Lord of Majesty, Bounty and Honor [88].

Everything in existence will perish, but the blessed Face of God will remain forever in His majesty, honor, and greatness.

The majesty and glory of God are invisible to the human eye. If we were to focus on parts of the universe that have not yet been explored, we will find out that the universe is expanding each moment. New galaxies and planets are being discovered. We can never know or reach the limits of the universe? This is the sign of the majesty, honor, and greatness of God that, regardless of our powerful telescopes and equipment, we are left with a mystery whenever we take an in-depth look at this universe.

One should then appreciate and strive to spiritually discover the beloved Creator through developing His love in one's heart.

When our hearts, bodies, minds, and souls become saturated with the love of God, the window to the invisible would open, and we could feel the blessed Face of God to whichever direction we turn our faces . Further, we would feel that **He is closer to us than our own souls.**

He is the most majestic and glorious in the whole of His creation and beyond. His bounties are infinite, and His actions are perfect and full of pure wisdom. All that is in the universe will perish one day but the Face of God, full of majesty, glory, and honor will remain forever.

His majesty and greatness keep Him over and above everything in existence for which He is praised and glorified by all creation. Some of His actions create fear because of the awesome force one can see in approaching twister, tornado or a hurricane.

Your Overwhelming Beauty

I asked, "Who are you like
In your overwhelming beauty?

He replied, "Only myself,
As I am quite Unique."

I am Love, Lover
And the Beloved

I am Beauty, I'm the Mirror,
And the Longing Eye.

Abu Said Abi Al Khayr

Greatness and Majesty belongs to God Alone

To show His greatness and majesty, He declares that all mankind are like beggars and needy in His sight. Anyone who claims this greatness, will be humiliated by the true owner of the majesty and glory. Even the powerful worldly kings and queens whom we address as your majesty are physically humbled and weakened when they get sick and old. Then they pray for their health, well-being and survival before the true majestic One. When the younger ones take over, no one remembers the older kings. This shows their majesty and power were temporary.

The seeker should show humility and pure devotion to the true King and seek His pleasure. He should avoid negative qualities of arrogance, false pride, hypocrisy, dishonesty, oppression and lies. Those, who realize the majesty and the honor of their Lord, God, receive strength and honor themselves.

If the Veil Falls from the Beloved's Face

If the veil would fall from the Beloved's Face,

Every atom would dance

Like it's stark raving mad

Every universe is intoxitaed from love's cup

But the cup is still full

Right to the brim.

Andalib Kashani

33

Discover the Life of Immortality

Abraham is still remembered after thousands of years.

God's love can make you experience immortality.

You go from this world like crossing the bridge to meet your Friend.

> *"There is no compulsion in religion.Verily, the Right Path has become distinct....grasp the most trustworthy handhold that will never break and God is All-Hearing, All-Knowing."*[89]

A man would be better off blind if he has no vision of the Friend.

"Where there is no vision of the Friend, a man would be better off blind. When your Friend is not everlasting, you had better avoid him."

Rumi

What the lover discovers because of his love and longing remains with him forever, and gives him a sense of immortality. This spiritual relationship and power you discover and develop with God stays with you forever. It does not become weak or diminished because of the aging process. In fact, your consciousness gains more vitality. It can even cure and heal the diseases and slow down the aging process. This spiritual power is permanent.

I remember my spiritual teacher mother Rabiah who was over 90 years of age could see things of this world and the next world at the same time. I was once talking to her of my late great grand father who was a spiritual man himself and she said to me, "he is standing and smiling right there" but I could not see him. She was seeing him through the inner power of faith and closeness to God.

This relationship is not a temporary position or power like that of the president of a country that is replaced after a certain number of years.

When God is pleased with you and loves you, you have achieved immortality. You are healed and you are able to heal others.

This Sorrow (This Love is He)

The sorrow
Of his love
Should become
Your habit

Then you'll discover
His love is sweet

Act like a human being
And embrace this sorrow

In the end
You will see
This love is HE.

Majd Al Din Taliba

You live forever in the hearts of people

Abraham, Moses, Jesus and Muhammad are still remembered by billions of people in the world today. Rumi, the great spiritual poet, passed away from this world eight hundred years ago, but people are eagerly reciting his poetry today? In fact he is one of the most popular poets in the world. There are many great spiritual people in the history who are always remembered by people.

Is that immortality? When you go away from this world, you live forever in the hearts of people in this world while the next world becomes paradise for you. You are satisfied with God, and He is satisfied with you. You are pleased with God, and He is pleased with you. You feel more closeness with Him than anything on this earth. That is true and everlasting success and real transformation.

There is a paradise in this world and in the next.

God has promised that He will make this world and the next like a paradise for those who have chosen to come closer to Him through their devotion, love and consciousness. Some people are praying and striving to go paradise, but they do not realize that they can make this world a paradise through experiencing the love and presence of the blessed Face of God which is a more powerful experience.

The Prophet Muhammad, while in solitude, used to experience the closeness and presence of God so intensely that his companions would come and join him, and he was not even aware of their presence. Later on, he used to come out of that very high state of closeness to a lower point of consciousness and realize the presence of his companions there. He would welcome them and ask when did they come and the answer was, "since long time."

"Is there any reward for excellent deeds other than excellence?" [90]

We can put it this way:

"Is there any reward for love of God other than His love?"

34

God Is All-Sufficient

**The satisfier of all your needs is ever
present and knows
all your needs even before you do.**

God is Omnipotent, Omniscient, all powerful, complete, and perfect in every respect. He is free from all wants and needs of living creatures. His attributes are beyond description and imagination. The entire universe and all the creatures living in it are in need of His support, commands, rewards, and blessings, which are always available to them.

God satisfies the needs of all the creations through means and channels that He might find most suitable. He is the sole recourse, the only source of support to free oneself of all troubles and pains and to receive all that one needs. His inexhaustible treasures are being distributed to all creatures in accordance with their needs. God knows your needs before you do and satisfies them. You should be thankful for whatever manner in which your needs are satisfied. For God is the all-knowing, generous and compassionate.

God is self-reliant but all existence depends on him.

"God! There is no god but Him, the Living, the Self-Existing, Eternal. Neither slumber can seize Him nor sleep. His are all things in the heavens and on earth."[91]

God does not depend on anything, nor does He require any support from anyone. He is the One who gives that which is necessary for the existence of everything. He has created the causes for the existence of everything and He is responsible for the survival of all things.

God's Divine Grace

Every atom of the created universe is constantly in need of divine grace, the special will of God that is present always, in different forms and strengths, in accordance with the need of everything in the universe. It is with that divine will that every atom obtains the cause for the satisfaction of its needs. If God cut off that favor for a split second, none would be able to survive. Billions of human beings can perish in a few minutes without the supply of oxygen.

Begging for a Glimpse

Both worlds are aglow
From the Light of the Friend

You hide in the world
Like the soul in a body

With yearning we are
Begging
For a glimpse
Of your beautiful Oneness

Please drop all those veils
From the sun of Your Face.

Shah Abu Ali Qalander

35

God is the Most Appreciative

When you thank Him, He bestows more favors on you.

"But if you count the favor of thy Lord, never will ye be able to count them." [92]

"What can God gain by your punishment, if you believe and are grateful? Nay, it is God who recognizes (good) and knows all things." [93]

"If you are grateful, I will increase (favors) unto you." [94]

God has shown that whether to choose the path of belief or disbelief or to be grateful or ungrateful is our choice. He would never compel us to His way. Truly grateful people recognize when God takes away their grief and suffering, and they turn to singing His praises.

God is appreciative because He recognizes our good intentions and actions. He is the one who repays a good deed with a much greater reward. Thankfulness is to return good with good. To be thankful is a duty of man towards God. He is the one who created you and poured all His bounties upon you. Should you not be grateful?

Blessed be the one who chooses to be thankful and spends generously in God's way whatever He bestows on him. Whatever we have is from God. The grateful person uses all his talents, strength, and wealth for God's pleasure. He invests for the care of human beings. God helps the thankful by increasing their wisdom, abilities, and fortunes.

There is but one God, Who gives all blessings to man and other creatures. His greatest gift is that He reveals His love and presence. In many tangible ways, He cares for man and provides for his growth and sustenance, in milk, fruits, honey, vegetation and cattle. In addition to physical growth, he provides opportunities for social, moral, and spiritual growth. These are signs for those who understand.

Now how can man thank God for His myriad favors?

They who seek zealously
the pleasure of God,

Most meekly tread
The path of His Love.

They do what God
asks them to do,

God does what
they wish Him do!

Rumi

Why does man then show ungratefulness by going after false gods and forgetting the true living and established Lord, God.?

Whoever is blessed with God's favors should offer his sincerest thanks to Him. Blessing is, as it were a wild beast, keep it under control by binding it with chains of thanks-offering.

"Then which are the favors of thy Lord, you deny." [95]

Thousand Thanks Due to Thee.

Without thee, O Beloved, I cannot rest,

Thy goodness towards one I cannot reckon.

Though every hair of my body becomes a tongue

A thousand parts of the thanks due to Thee I cannot tell!

Rumi

36

God declares:
"I Am the Time"

"Sons of Adam inveigh against (the vicissitudes of) Time, and I am Time, in My hand is the night and the day."[96]

"By the Time, Verily, man is in loss, except those who believe and do righteous deeds, and (join together) in the mutual teaching of the Truth, and of patience and constancy."[97]

Do you know how much of your life is gone and how much is remaining? Becoming conscious of the loving Creator and the time that is remaining in my life allows me to wake up with a sense of urgency and reorganize the priorities in my life to achieve my life's full potential.

God gives us a new life with each new breath. You live by breaths.

You live from one breath to the next breath. Your real life is not in years but in moments. Your life ends with each moment, and you get a new lease on life with the next moment. There are some people who do not receive the next breath and pass away. Those who love God say that with each breath we should thank Him. They might be doing their daily work and carrying on their businesses and work, but they always remember God. I feel as though God is saying:

You can still bring a revolution in your life

"I created the day and night and created a sense of time for your life, but for Me, yesterday, today, and tomorrow are as today. I am not bound by time or space or anything because I am the time. You, however, have a specific and fixed term. You live a pure and joyful life in which you can have comforts, live your best life, have the best foods but remember your generous and bountiful Lord, God."

"Two favors are treated unjustly by most people health and free time."

(Tradition - by Abne Abbas)

Divine Oneness

Is like being in sunshine.
Nourish the Soul
Desire the loaf
Which nourishes the soul?

Seek the knowledge
Which can never?
Be written
In words

Desire the secret
Hidden in the hearts
Of God's friends
Even beyond the grasp
Of angels.

Rumi

"But you went so deep in the worldly life that you didn't appreciate the value of your time and your life. You took care of the world. I gave you the gift of life and the time as a favor and a blessing for doing great things. You can still awaken yourself from sleep. You can still soar above the heavens. You can still bring a spiritual revolution in your life."

I am the Time. I am the source of all life.

God's statement can be interpreted as: I am the time. I am the source of all life, love, light, mercy, grace, forgiveness, compassion, treasures, nourishment, and healing. I am established on the great throne and I am present everywhere in the universe, in the oceans, in the galaxies, in the worlds, in the places of worship, and in the pure hearts. I am always before you each moment of your life.

The true success for you is to develop an excellent character based on life models like those of Abraham, Moses, Jesus, Muhammad and others like them.

The Blessed Face of God is always before us everywhere.

God is present with us through His awareness,
God is present with us through His knowledge,
God is present with us through His wisdom,
God is present with us through His sight,
God is present with us through His hearing,
God is present with us through His greatness,
God is present with us through His closeness and
God is present with us through His power and energy.

You are on a journey of life. Know the true significance of your time and surrender to the real power before you now. This moment can make the difference for your prosperity in this world and the next world. Fall in love with your loving Creator. How long will you keep Him waiting? You have to meet Him one day.

Time is leaving you behind each moment. This is the moment so make the decision. Change your life and start on the path of love.

The Mirror of the King's Beauty

The Divine Book's imprint
Is nothing but you?

The mirror of the King's Beauty
Is nothing but you?

Not a thing in this world
Is outside of you.

Whatever you're seeking
You'll find it in you.

Baba Afzal Kashani

They say they just come into this world and time takes their life

There are a lot of people who do not believe in God; instead, they say they just come into this world and time takes their lives and they pass away from here. Some say they just become energy when they leave this World.

God says that He is the Time and He will take account of all actions. There is the life of paradise which is an infinite life and there is no dying in that life. There is also the opposite place. He says He has kept rewards for the fortunate ones which their eyes (they) cannot imagine.

37

God's Justice is Perfect

His court is open twenty-four/seven in the universe.

His is the perfect justice that is opposite of tyranny. When God created the first man and the angels suggested that this man would create bloodshed and oppression, God replied that they did not know what He knew and that His true servants would obey His rules and love Him. One should never become a slave to another man but become a servant of God.

Tyranny causes destruction and suffering. Justice secures peace, safety, balance, and harmony. God is the just one, and the scales of justice are in the heavens invisible to our eyes. Tyranny and violence in any form should be avoided. One should surrender only to God who gives us inner and outer peace.

God wants us to love Him and our fellow human beings

If you love Him, then you should not kill the innocent people. He would not accept any excuse of you hurting, injuring or killing innocent people. Everybody has just as much right to life as yourself.

Produce the life back which you took away unlawfully

The perfect justice will require that you produce the life back which you took away unlawfully: you had no right to do that. The justice requires that you can hurt the one who hurt you to the extent of your injury. Now the victim is asking for his rights in the court of God. Also think of the pain you caused to the victim's family, relatives and friends?

Walk in My Light...

Once I was here,
But now "I" am not:

If there's really a "me,"
It could only be you

If any robe warms
And encompasses me now
That very robe
It could only be you

In the way of your love
Nothing was left
Neither body nor soul

If I have any body
If I have any soul
Then, without question, it could only be you.

Ala al Dawla Simnani

If you killed and tortured an innocent person unjustly, then you can receive the same kind of treatment as you gave to others. We have to exercise self-control and not hurt anyone who has not done any harm to us due to anger or some other harmful emotion. Do not remain in any illusion of doing whatever you wish and expect God to be on your side. Many judges who sometimes let the criminal go free or sentenced innocent people, might be called to answer in that great court. God is always on the side of the innocent victim and not on the side of the oppressor. That is His Perfect justice.

"Take your account daily before your account is taken"[98]

The universe is subject only to His laws.

This is the mystic record, the eternal law, according to which everything seen and unseen is ordered and regulated. The simplest things in nature are subject to God's laws. The fresh and the withered, the living and the lifeless—nothing is outside the plan of His creation.

The path of love is beyond the universal laws. How did Jesus walk on water? No human being can walk on water except through the power of faith and Jesus had that faith. God's love and your strong faith can make you walk on water and soar above the heavens. You can strengthen your faith through worship, service, fasting and meditation.

38

God Creates All Motion and Power

He is regulating the universe by His command

"He is the Omnipotent over His servants. He is Wise and All-Knowing." [99]

Not even a particle of dust can move without the permission of Almighty God. Motion is also the creation of God and is not acquired by the strength of power. Power and motion are both attributes of God. Any power and motion happening in the universe is from the Originator. The scientists have discovered that there is a command and control center and positive force that is holding and controlling the entire universe.

His power enables the movements of men.

When you see movement you know there is life. Every event in the world is happening because of His power and energy. All the actions of His servants maintain a connection with His power. All motions are connected with the power and energy from God. The seeker knows that God alone has gifted him and everything else with attributes of power and motion. All major elements in the universe are like puppets whose movements are made possible through strings by their Maker.

The entire universe could cease functioning in a second.

Just like a powerful vehicle that weighs tons can come to a standstill when it runs out of fuel, the universe could stop functioning without the energy and power provided by God.

With Him are the keys of the invisible and only He knows them.

Creation's Witness

At time's beginning,
That beauty

Which polished creation's mirror?
Caressed every Atom
With a hundred thousand suns.

But this glory
Was never witnessed;

When the human eye emerged,
Only then was He known.

Mirza Abdal Qadir

39

God is the Most Trustworthy

Whoever puts his trust in God, He will be sufficient for him.

"He provides you from where you cannot even imagine."[101]

God says that the true believers put their trust only in Him. When they place their trust in God, He provides for all their needs in ways they cannot even imagine. He prepares a special way to lead them out of all difficulties. God knows how to accomplish His purpose, and He has established a measure for all things.

Everything will perish and His Face will remain forever.

"Whatsoever is on (this earth) will perish. And the Face of your Lord, Full of Majesty, Bounty and Honor will remain forever."[102]

The most magnificent works of man such as building planes, ships, empires, the wonders of science and art, and the splendors of human glory or intellect will all pass away. The most magnificent objects in nature like mountains, valleys, the sun, and the moon will all pass away in their appointed time. Only God will remain forever with all His glory, majesty, bounty, essence, honor, power, love, mercy, compassion, forgiveness, and generosity.

Hold His handhold

Turn your face then toward the true God

You should realize that only God can provide you with true guidance and consolation. One should hold His Handhold of mercy and turn to the blessed Face of God.

God is the source of all solutions for mankind.

Discoveries and innovative solutions occur through His inspiration.

He eliminates all obstacles and opens up new avenues and opportunities for us. He has solutions to every imaginable problem or challenge facing mankind today. He does not force His will on anyone.

Shine a reflection of Your Face in this world

Dangle a stress from your disheveled curls

And you'll evict the monks from their monasteries

Shine a reflection of Your Face in this world

And even the idols will kneel down in prostration.

Ruzbiban Bagli

If we are keen and keep the doors of our minds and hearts open, his words of wisdom will produce solutions for us.

If anyone closes a door on you, God can open new doors and opportunities. If God does not open the doors of His blessings, no force can open those doors. But God is always here to remove the obstacles in your way. You just need to make some effort. Believe in God, put your trust in Him and love Him.

He solves all problems and makes way for ease in difficulties.

We remember Him only on special occasions mostly when we are in difficulties. We try to impose our will on others. We dictate our own solutions and rules, which create injustice and imbalance.

He has the keys to all the treasurers in the universe. There is a treasure of everything in God's kingdom.

He has the keys to the secrets of knowledge, wisdom, and all the spiritual and material treasures in the universe.

As human beings, we pass through states, problems, and things that one cannot see through without outside help. Some are material things like professions, jobs, gains, possessions, places and friends. There are also hearts with sadness and minds tied up in doubts or questions they are unable to answer. So turn to God and with His permission, you will see when He opens the closed door.

We can open the doors of treasures by becoming generous to our fellow human beings who are poor, illiterate, and weak. We should avoid hurting anyone, being oppressive and abusive, so that we merit His mercy and bounty.

Every Name that Exists

No atom exists
That is apart
From the sun

Every raindrop is from
The same ancient sea

Has no one a name
For this ultimate Truth

Every name that exists
Is already owned
By that Truth.

Dard Shikub

40

The Secret to Inner Happiness and Contentment

Remembrance of God is the greatest

"And those who believe and whose hearts find contentment in the remembrance of God:Verily, in the remembrance of God do hearts find contentment (peace)." [103]

Remember Me - God

I am as My servant thinks I am.
I am with him when he makes mention of Me.
If he makes mention of Me to himself, I make mention of him to Myself, and If he makes mention of Me in an assembly, I make mention of him in an assembly. If he comes closer to me one step,

> *I draw near to him an arm's length; and if he draws near to Me an arm's length, I draw near to him a fathom's length. And if he comes to Me walking, I go to him at speed.* [104]

When we remember God, He remembers us. This is such a simple equation. He says the remembrance of God will create peace, contentment and happiness in our hearts. This act of remembering God can save us from fear, worries, anxieties, negative thoughts, and even depression.

I know when God remembers me. When I remember Him, He remembers me.

"If you remember Me, I shall remember you. Be thankful to Me and do not become ungrateful (disbeliever) to Me."[105]

God inspires us to remember Him. He says He will remember us when we remember Him. One spiritual scholar said that he knows when God remembers him. When asked how he knows, he said that he firmly believes that when he remembers God, He remembers him according to His words.

When you focus and think of God with love, He too thinks of you with love. The key point is that we have to have firm belief in God and in His words. God says that there are people who have fear and love of their Lord and their hearts tremble and they have goose bums when they recite His verses. Then their skins and hearts soften to the remembrance of God. That is the sign of true guidance.

Manifestation of the Divine Greatness

Self's realization can result in the
Manifestation of the Divine Greatness

Self's realization can result in the
Manifestation of the excellent character of the Prophet

The earth, heavens, the Divine Throne and the Divine Court
Lie within the bounds of the true Self

Sir Dr. Mohammad Iqbal,
The Poet of the East

The intense love and feeling the presence of God are the desirable states one can achieve in this world. We should strive to remember our loving Creator as this could open channels of communications between us and God. We should surrender to Him in obedience, service, and love, and remember Him with our tongues, minds, and hearts all the time while carrying on our daily tasks.

41

Contemplation of God and His Creation

"One hour's contemplation is better than eighty years of worship."

This is the saying of the Prophet Muhammad to show the importance of contemplation in God Who says that in the creation of the heavens and the earth, and in the alternation of day and night, there are indeed signs for men of understanding. Upon reflection, the changing of seasons from spring to summer to autumn and winter reveal the hand of God.

God appreciates people who remember Him standing, sitting, and while lying on their sides, and then they engage in contemplation of God and the creation of this vast universe. They realize and acknowledge that God has not created this wonderful universe in vain. They celebrate His praises and glorify Him seeking His salvation from the difficulties of this world and the hereafter.

"And those who will strive in Us, We shall open the doors for them."[106]

There is so much benefit in the constant remembrance of God and contemplation in Him. We should contemplate in His essence, His attributes, and His words. When contemplating the words of God and traditions, the creation, and mankind, you should ask yourself:

Who am I?

Who am I?
Where did I come from?
Why am I in this world?
What is the purpose of my life?
Who is my Creator?
Am I on the right way?
Am I realizing my life's full potential?

Where do I go from here?

There is not a single question which does not have an answer if we are determined and persevere to find the truth.

Manifestation of the Divine Grace

Self's realization can result in the
Manifestation of the Divine Greatness

Self's realization can result in the
Manifestation of the excellent character of the Prophet

The earth, heavens, the Divine Throne and the Divine Court
Lie within the bounds of the true Self

Sir Dr. Mohammad Iqbal,
The Poet of the East

42

God is the Most Forgiving and the Best Protector

God is infinitely forgiving.

God can turn your sins into good deeds.

God is full of forgiveness. He expects us to strive for excellence, but He knows we can make mistakes during the course of our lives. He is always before us to accept our repentance. It is not necessary for anyone to look for an intermediary to arrange repentance. You can go directly to God to confess and ask for forgiveness as He is close to you.

He is the most forgiving and merciful. He accepts repentance and cleanses any burdens or sins you might carry. You can confess your sins directly to Him and repent to Him. You will be surprised by His loving response to you. He says:

If your sins are like oceans, My mercy is greater than the oceans

He says:"If your sins are as much as the oceans, My mercy is far greater than the oceans. I can forgive you."[22]

God loves those who repent to Him.

He is God of supreme generosity that exceeds human imagination.

"Except those who repent and believe and do righteous deeds, for those, God will convert their sins into good deeds, and God is the Most-Forgiving, the Most Merciful."[109]

He can forgive you again and again as He is full of pity and kindness. Should you repent to Him for your sins and make a firm commitment for doing righteous deeds and actions, He can not only blot your sins but turn your sins into good deeds. No one on this earth can give you that kind of guarantee except your loving Creator because He cares for you and does not want any harm come to you or your family.

God Protects all Creation from Harm

"There is no soul but has a guard (angel) protecting over it.."
[107]

God is the best protector of His creations. He safeguards and protects through knowledge and wisdom. He planted the protection and security mechanism in our bodies. He has given us an instinct for survival and continuity. He has taught and shown us that if we drink poison we can die or touching the live electric wire can give us life-threatening shock.

The authorities place signs of danger over medicine, electric poles, and many hazardous things to prevent accidents. God has appointed angels to protect us from all kinds of harm and these angels defeat the snares of the accursed Satan. Also, you have the knowledge given to you by God to teach your children about safety and harmful things.

43

God is the Only One Who Truly Exists

**He is working from behind the veils.
All you see in the universe is His presence and
His handiwork.**

The bubble of water looks beautiful but then it just bursts as if there was nothing. Alexander the Great's empire was known all over the world and then it disappeared over time. The Roman empire created awe in the world through wars and then it crumbled on the face of the earth.

We have not been able to figure out exactly how old the universe is, but the estimates are in billions of years. The universe is expanding each moment. The world can come to an end instantly if the nuclear weapons stored by nations are used in a world-war scenario. This world is and everything in it is temporary. Spiritually speaking, temporary things do not have a real existence. So the spiritually wise people say that only God truly exists as He is ever-lasting.

Some day everything will perish but the blessed Face of God will remain forever.

Whatever you continuously focus on can expand and divulge its secrets before you. If you reflect, meditate, and contemplate in God, you will find Him close. If the leaf of a tree can speak, it will tell you who created it. When I go for a walk, I see the blue sky and sometimes pinkish and reddish light around the setting sun. I see various kinds of plants, flowers and trees. Who created this green carpet of grass under your feet and different kinds of trees around you? Who designed and fashioned the leaves and branches, some tall and high and some spread widely? Who creates the changing colors of the sunset and the blue sky and the heavens above? God.

The summer heat is driving a deer out of the forest to get to the nearby pond. I feel the evening breeze and hear the noise of birds flying overhead. Because of the recent rain, frogs are singing in groups; bugs and small insects are swarming. You can see the hand of God in everything He has created and it is a proof of His existence, presence and power. Some things are created directly and some through the hands of men.

Through devotion and focus in God the seeker reaches a point, where he feels His presence everywhere and the doors of knowledge are opened to him. Further, the seeker feels that God is the only One who truly exists as He is the everlasting one.

Knowledge of God and the divine aspects came to be associated with the world of creation or phenomena. He is the first and the last and the outward and the inward. He knows all things, and He is present in every direction and every loving heart.

You will get closer and closer to God as your Faith intensifies

After this secret you will have to strive to keep this knowledge always in focus. In other words, you should be able to perpetually feel the intimate presence of God within and around you every moment. Your forgetfulness of God should disappear, so that you may be blessed perpetually with this feeling of His presence and gradually you may experience a complete effacement in the essence of God. You will start understanding how everything happening is connected and intended to further strengthen your belief in His presence. You will get closer and closer to God as your faith intensifies more and more. If you contemplate more, you will find His presence close to everything in this world.

44

God Says, "Be" and It Is!

God is the originator of actions and movements.

He has created the universe as a mirror to reflect His essence.

"Verily, His Command, when He intends a thing, is only that He says to it, "Be!" and it is!"[110]

One great spiritual teacher Abdul Qadir Jilani of Baghdad said: "That when the one who loves God and whom God also loves, says, "Be' for something to happen God says, 'it is.' The seeker only wishes for something to happen and it does happen. In that state, he can change the course of a hurricane if he so wishes.

Nothing can withstand the power of his or her faith

Nothing can withstand the power of his faith and this state comes due to his intense love and faith in God. He inspires other people with compassion and love.

God thinks, designs, plans, and creates just by the word " Be." All these functions happen in an instant. God fashions, originates, and creates a cycle and system for each living creature instantly. This includes its beginning, its end, and how is it going to sustain, the system of nourishment for that creation, survival, and its fruition.

He can create people like us or even better than us.

"Is not He who created the heavens and the earth, able to create the like of them? Yes, indeed! He is the All-Knowing, Supreme."[11]

One can hardly visualize the extent and nature of God's power of creation. Imagine how He created a dynamic universe within the human body and limitless universe all around us. Imagine how he created gravity and the vacuum of space. Consider also hurricanes, tornadoes, and earthquakes—could any human power control these disasters? God is the One who allows all movement and actions in the universe. We do not see His blessed hand doing His work but we only see the finished product or action.

He is the only One who has infinite power, Who bestows His gifts to us and Who allows our survival and the survival of the entire universe from one moment to the next.

He pushes the switch for action to originate. Without His permission and ability not even a leaf can move. God is the only creator of energy. We can transfer the energy from one form to another like from coal to electricity, but we cannot create the energy. We cannot even see the electricity, but when we see a television set working we know the electricity is there. We are unable to see how the visual images (with sound) are converted into electrical signals, transmitted and displayed electronically on television screen. If somebody were to give a lecture on how this electronic transmission system works, it will take a long time and many people will not understand. But if the person simply switches on the television set, people can watch the world news and believe in how this amazing system works.

We deny the presence of God because we don't see Him physically

Similarly, we are unable to see the light and the presence of God, so we simply deny His existence. However, if you can develop God's love in your heart which will start receiving spiritual signals and displaying them on the screen of your heart, you will believe in how you can spiritually feel His presence and even communicate with Him. You will see the spiritual pictures and believe in His presence just like the people who, in the earlier example, saw the world news on the television screen and believed in the system.

The universe is a mirror to manifest God's creative power

God has created the universe as a mirror to manifest His power and energy. His power of invention and creation are only conditioned by one thing: His will. If He wills, He can destroy and recreate everything.

Billions of celestial bodies are manifestation of His presence.

He says look up in the heavens: "Do you see any defect in the heavens above?" "Your eyes will return without finding any fault in the heavens above or in the stars."

We feel awe when we contemplate in God's creation—the intricate and elegant way everything works together—plants, animals, and nature. Consider how wonderfully complex man is and yet how little man needs to do to control the working of his body. Who can produce such a miracle other than God?

45

God's Supreme Perfection

"Blessed is He in Whose Hand is the dominion, and He is able to do all things..........Who has created the seven heavens one above another, you will see no defect in the universe."[112]

He is perfect and free of restrictions and limitations. His perfection has no limits. All excellence is His. God's name is the Essence and encompasses all qualities, attributes of perfection. God's name signifies the qualities of unity and oneness. Praise be to Him, the Creator, the First and the Last. He is the doer of whatever He wills. He guides His servants toward the true path of His love.

To see the proof of His perfection, we can look at the perfection in His creation. God created cows that eat grass and hay and produce milk that is consumed by man. We drink milk from our infancy to the old age. But we rarely appreciate how God created this source of nourishment for us all. God says do you see how He creates milk from the belly of the cow when the cow eats grass and the milk is produced from in between the blood and the waste and there is no contamination. How can grass turn into white nourishing milk? An amazing miracle!

All fruit trees and vegetable plants produce different types of fruits and vegetables with different colors even though they took in the same water. Look at the hardness of the coconut shell and consider that it is created from water. How can the water turn into rock-like shell. How the date has a hard pit in the middle and the walnut have rock-like shells around? These are only a few of the miracles of God.

God is pure and the source of all purity.

"He is God, than whom there is no other god, the Sovereign Lord, Pure free from faults, defects, weakness or imperfections."
113

God is the most pure and devoid of all blemishes, shortcomings, weaknesses, heedlessness, and faults. He is free from failures, forgetfulness, absentmindedness, slumber and sleep.

He is the Creator who bears no resemblance to the created. Even the most perfect creatures have something lacking in their essence, attributes, actions, judgments, or words. God almighty is eternal. We must praise God for His perfection and remember to avoid attributing any qualities that are defective or any temporal imperfect state to God.

Once our hearts are purified, cleansed, and perfected through devotion and love of God, they will become like the houses of

God where He is exalted, honored, praised, remembered and contemplated each day.

God Is Unique

"Say: He is God who is One" [100]

God is unique and indivisible. He is unique in creation and unrivalled in every new creation. He has neither equal nor any partner in His essence, His attributes, His actions, His commands and His powers. He fixed the provision and lives of all the being and nothing can escape from His presence. His presence and might are infinite.

The entire universe is moving, existing, and running because of the energy from the source, the light, the wisdom, and the power of Godʼs attributes and qualities. He is the original source of all energy which is light and which is one of His most powerful attributes. When you see light, you should remember that God is the source of all light. He provides light to all of His creation and this is His uniqueness.

When you focus on His attributes, qualities and actions, you will discover His uniqueness in everything. No two blades of grass are the same and no two finger tips are the same. He creates everything unique. That is standard and His stamp.

46

The Doer of What He Pleases

He can make you laugh or cry.

People go through their lives according to the choices they make. Nothing happens by chance. There are cosmic laws and order. There is a system and wisdom in this universe. People call the reality by different names.

A piece of wood or steel is just a piece of wood or steel with whatever atoms and characteristics God has implanted in it. Everything is under the control of the rule of God. He can make you laugh and make you cry based on your choices in life. He can make you sick or healthy, rich or poor according to your choices. You can never blame Him.

I recently heard of a very wealthy man who had billions of dollars worth of assets. He lost all his wealth and is now in the prison due to financial fraud. There is another person in the news who claims he was homeless and is now a billionaire. There is a country in Africa engaged in years of warfare among its citizens. Beautiful young men and women are dying sometimes due to coming in the cross-fire. The hostile groups can decide to control their emotions, turn their hatred into love, embrace each other and bring peace in a matter of few weeks but it requires self-sacrifice. They can start the journey of prosperity, healing and happiness any time they wish. It is their choice.

This world is like a Divine department store. If you go to department of His generosity, you will find it there, and you can freely use it. If you go to His department of forgiveness, it is available there, and you can use it. If you visit the department of love, you can use it too. If you go to the department of compassion, you can display the same towards all people.

In fact, all you see in this universe is a reflection of God's attributes.

God is able to do all things:

God can make you Laugh and cry

"He makes you laugh and makes you cry." [114]
"And will ye laugh. And not weep." [115]

God can Heal you or let you have Sickness

"When I become sick. He heals and restores my health." says Abraham. [116]

God can give you life or take it away

"He gives you life and takes it away." [117]

God can make you Rich or poor

"He makes you rich and can make you poor." [118]

Universe in His hand

"The entire universe and creation is in His Blessed hand and whoever wishes, can come to meet his Lord." [119]

God wants to purify you

"Whoever wants can purify oneself." [120]

God is pleased with you

"He is pleased with you and you are pleased with Him." [121]

He is established on His throne above heaven and everywhere

"He is established on His throne, above the heavens and everything." [122]

He is nevertheless very near to us and everything.

Have I not made the earth a couch and created you male and female? [123]

God has made the earth like a couch and mountains like tents. He has created all human beings of two sexes, male and female, for each other's comfort. He has created night for sleep and rest, and the day to seek livelihood through business and employment. He created seven heavens above and placed therein a burning lamp and sent down rainwater in abundance from clouds so that corn, herbs, vegetables, fruits, and trees can spring up from the earth. All these are miracles of the loving God for human beings and other creatures. His miracles are taking place each moment.

47

God wants us to take our own Accounts

You can judge yourself before you are judged. Each person has an invisible video with him

This world is based on the principle of accountability of what we do and say. Accountability is very crucial in life. If someone is seriously listening to his own thoughts and watching his actions, he can determine whether there is any injustice or harm being done through his tongue, hands, mind, or body. He could stop his negative behavior.

Self-evaluation, self-control and accountability are at the heart of character building. This way we can keep a watch on ourselves to determine if we are being controlled by our egos or we are in control.

> *"Read your record: Sufficient is your own self, this day, to take account of yourself."*[124]

You are the police, accused, and the prosecutor Judge your own self.

God has appointed angels as guards and watchers with us, one angel on the right and one on the left. The right angel records positive things and the left angel records the negatives. We can be our own judges. This means to forgive people right here and have them forgive us. You watch what you say and what you do and thus be free and safe each day.

Our skins and body organs might speak as witnesses against us that they saw us abusing ourselves and creating suffering or pain to our fellow human beings. We were arrogant and went against our own souls, committed immoral acts and crimes without fearing anybody. There can also be positive witnesses telling you were so kind and loving to other human beings regardless of their origin, race or creed. As has been mentioned before, God is full of forgiveness and accepts our repentance.

Take your own account, before your account is taken. [125]

It is better to remain silent than to engage in vain talk, gossip, or false news or stories without first doing due investigation. Spreading of bad news is inappropriate; that is why, someone said silence is golden. The Prophet Muhammad advised his companions to take their own accounts before their accounts are taken. He told them to avoid vain talk, gossiping, backbiting and oppressing others.

48

God's Will, Words, and Wise Actions

God's will, words, and actions are based on wisdom and compassion. What God wills comes into being. Nothing can happen without His will and power. Actions take place according to His will or permission.

Not a glance of the eye is outside His knowledge.

Not a glance of the eye or a stray sudden thought is outside His will. He does what He wills. There is none to stop His command. There are no obstacles to it. There is no refuge from Him except in Him. None can follow His command without His will. If all mankind wants to remove an atom from its proper place, it will be impossible without God's will. His will lies naturally in His attributes. There is no precedence or subsequence of any event from its appointed time. When you know God, you can discover some secrets of how His will works. He lets you have knowledge of why hurricanes, floods, tsunamis and earth-quakes devastate certain regions. Natural events take place through the will of God.

When I worked in one American global corporation, we used to prepare five-year business plans based on assumptions of economic, political, and social environments in the various regions of the world. These plans included purchase of land, construction of plants and recruitment of employees in the future. Each year the plans were revised significantly because of changing economic and political conditions. In some cases, the expansion and construction of new plants had to be abandoned because of political changes and the resulting economic instability. The corporations and governments have to keep changing plans due to new global challenges.

The unforeseeable events cannot happen without the will of God. There are millions of instances that clearly show how God's will is functioning in the universe but man is not conscious of it. Ordinary people find events when they actually happen, the spiritual people have advance knowledge of these events as I have learnt from my personal experience due to closeness of my loving Creator.

The wise words of God

The pure hearts can understand the words of God contained in the holy books. The Torah, Bible, and Quran are His sacred books that He gave to His messengers Moses, Jesus, and Muhammad respectively. Each book contains wisdom according to the times of its revelation and the future. One should really try to understand the inner meanings of the words of God with an open mind as it is a serious matter to find out what God wants from us. A person can receive guidance from these revelations if he has an open mind. A person can get a negative impression from the study of revelation if he has the negative intention to find fault. That is why God says in Quran, "Many people have been guided by the Quran and many have been misguided by it (due to their misunderstanding of it)."

You can hear God speak to you through His words

There is always a hidden spiritual meaning in the words of God. Some people are in haste and just look at the apparent meaning and start advocating actions which can bring ruin to them and others. That was not God's intention as He is full of wisdom, love and peace.

I feel as if God is saying, "Yes, I am close to you.

God can speak without sound or voice. It is eternal, ancient, and self-existing unlike the talks of a created being. God's words, speech, statements, commands, and truths are pure wisdom for daily use. He can use any instrument and language in the universe as a means of communication to His creations. For example, it is mentioned in the Quran that when God **spoke to Moses on the mountain of Sinai, the voice was coming from behind the tree and there was a fire. God was speaking from behind the veils.**

God is wise in all His actions.

He is the source of all creative actions. He is wise in His actions. He created everything in its best form. Whatever exists in the world derives from His power of creativity.

He sent messengers and prophets to convey His wisdom to ensure happiness and ease for the human beings. He gave us miracles and conveyed His injunctions and prohibitions to guide us all.

49

God Bestows Favors Unconditionally

He pours unlimited favors and gifts on us

When we do someone a favor, we expect something in return, at least a thank you. If someone ignores us after receiving a benefit or gift from us, we say that person is ungrateful or even arrogant. But God is the most benevolent. When He bestows benefits, favors, and gifts on you or accepts your calls for help, He does it unconditionally and without expecting anything in return.

If we thank Him and are appreciative, He is pleased and gives us more, but He is not in need of our thanks. It is only fair that we thank Him for His countless favors. When the most generous gives to you, no one can prevent that good from coming to you.

God has implanted the quality of generosity in people who also like to donate and give gifts to their fellow human beings. Man has limited resources to share, but God's treasures are limitless.

Should we not then thank God and be grateful for His continued favors? In some countries, farmers look to the sky for rain after planting the seeds. They almost always get their wish. How much thanks are due to God who gives infinitely to all His creations?

50

God is the King and Ruler of the Universe

"And to God belongs the Rule of the heavens and the earth, and in the alternation of night and day, there are indeed signs for men of understanding (knowledge)."[127]

"So Exalted be God, the true King, the Truth."[128]

He is the owner of the universe and absolute ruler of all creation. He is the Creator of His kingdom, which He created from nothing. Only He knows the size of His kingdom.

God is the ruler of this world and the next. On the Day of Judgment, He will announce: "who is the ruler today." There will be no answer; Then He will declare that He is the Only Ruler and King.

In the world, one's deeds are planted, and on the Day of Judgment, the rewards will be reaped. Everyone will reap the results according to what seeds he has planted by way of his actions. People can also receive rewards for their good work right in this world.

To the extent of his consciousness, devotion, and obedience, one may expect to be rewarded by one's master.

51

God Is Full of Pity and Kindness

He is full of clemency for mankind.

"He is full of pity for all mankind. He is not in need of His creation. His Mercy and Clemency are infinite." [129]

God says that when the heavens observe the oppression on this earth against the innocent people and wrongful actions and sins, the heavens want to fall. When the earth observes oppression, violence against the weak and innocent people, it wants to open up and take in all oppressors. But God holds the earth from sinking in and the heavens from falling due to His mercy and pity for all mankind. [130]

God observes actions of the arrogant and rebellious among mankind but because of His infinite patience, He gives people opportunities to reflect and evaluate their own actions so they can repent and follow the path of love and compassion. He relents and gives ample time to people so they can amend their evil ways, and turn back to the right way. He withholds His punishment and chooses to forgive many because of His infinite mercy and clemency.

God says all birds, animals and plants are but communities like us. The animals do not have intellect like human beings, but they do care for their offsprings. How do birds build nests and search for food ? They are not destructive to their communities like men. Unlike these beautiful animals, man builds dangerous weapons so he can destroy his fellow human beings in the shortest possible time. He forgets that his Creator is watching.

Can we not become better than plants, animals and birds?

Can we, human beings, not become better than plants, animals and birds that take care of their communities? We have so many nuclear weapons in the world today that we can destroy all humanity many times over. But why should we destroy God's creation against His wish? He can destroy humanity Himself if He so desires.

52

God is the Giver of True Peace

"The Beneficent Lord sends peace, blessing, and salutation to the believers in Paradise." [130]

God rewards the believers with the peace and joy of the wished for paradise. He is the one who saves the believing servants from all dangers, bringing them peace and blessing of paradise. He is persisting, uninterrupted, unfaltering and is eternal.

Those who find the peace and security of God in their hearts believe in and depend on Him for all their affairs; they know that by the grace of that blessed name they will be saved from all dangers and difficulties. When they are saved from a danger by someone, they see the real Savior.

The seeker is always striving to be in peace. He sees with the wisdom of God and avoids any situation where he can become dragged into some unpleasantness. But he is not afraid of getting dragged into discomforts and challenges while performing the service to God or His fellow human beings.

Solitude, silence, and smiling.

"Most of the sufferings and difficulties come to a person on account of what he says and talks with his tongue."[131]

One can learn the attributes of solitude, silence and smiling from the great messengers of God. They inspired mankind towards remembrance of God, contemplation, self-evaluation, and ways and means of achieving closeness to God

The Prophet Muhammad used to go outside the city and confine himself in a cave named Hira on top of a mountain called mountain of light. It was a few miles away from the city of Mecca and was a very lonely place. He used to keep fasts and spend days in solitude and contemplation in God. He had not as yet received revelation from God to declare the message of His Oneness.

God says that the prophet does not say anything from his own self but speaks only what is inspired by Him. The Prophet had the disposition of maintaining silence and always smiling.

Today, people are going through suffering and hardships all over the world not because there is shortage of food and water but because of improper distribution of these resources and man-made political problems and violence. There is more food wasted daily in the wealthy western and eastern countries that it could feed all the hungry people in the world. That can happen only when we become caring people.

Nothing is impossible if you have the will and focus in God

We should inspire wisdom, knowledge, compassion, care, concern, love, and mercy in the hearts of people today and spread the light in the world. This process will create awareness, contentment, happiness, patience and love. The material shortages and poverty will disappear from the face of the earth along with all suffering, diseases, and ignorance.

You can join us to spread the light all over the world

This book has been written with the goal, mission and purpose of spreading the light of knowledge and love to remove ignorance and darkness. You, too, can consider joining us in this great team effort and make a positive difference in the world.

53

God is the Perfect Artist and Designer

God is the perfect designer and artist who gives everything the most unique and colorful form. He shapes everything in the perfect fashion. No two things are the same, including your fingerprints. Each and every creation is a choice creation, an expression of God's infinite beneficence and wisdom.

God's attributes of perfect harmony and shaper of unique beauty are manifested in the nearest and liveliest way in human beings. Man makes, builds and shapes many beautiful and useful things. He fashions and designs things utilizing that attribute gifted to him by God who is the perfect designer.

As an example, see how perfectly God designed the human eye, which automatically closes or blinks when anything comes near to the eyes. Look at the colors or the iris from black, brown, green, blue, and hazel. The eyes guide all actions of man.

God maintains perfect harmony and balance in the universe.

"Do you see any incongruity in the Creation of the Beneficent? Then Look again, can you see any defect or disorder." [132]

He creates all things in perfect proportion. He maintains His creation in perfect order not only each thing being harmonious within itself, but everything in the universe in harmony with everything else.

The functions of one and all depend upon each other. This harmony that is in your nature should be manifested in your life. God gave you intelligence to help you get to know Him, so we should seek Him

The Creator of gravity makes sure things do not deviate

God challenges us that we should probe the heavens to find any defect. We can take all our scientists up in the space to do research and find any deficiency in the creations of the heavens. They will find none. The entire universe is in total balance and equilibrium from every angle.

54

God's Infinite Vastness

The universe does not encompass God but He encompasses it.

His kingdom is beyond limits and boundaries.

God's vastness is beyond imagination. His knowledge, mercy, power, generosity and all other beautiful attributes are infinite. His vastness is infinite in every aspect - love, forgiveness, closeness and everything. The all-reaching vastness of God is reflected in men of great knowledge, in men of great riches and generosity that help the needy. In men of compassion, gentleness and patience whose far-reaching justice inspires great confidence and the limitless good qualities. The wrongs and sins of men are like a drop of dirt in the vastness of God's ocean of tolerance, forgiveness, and mercy.

God is beyond your imagination physically, yet so close spiritually.

When you look at the full moon, it is so bright and looks so close. It is actually very far from us. The nuclear plant that generates electric power is hundreds of miles away from our house; yet, the electricity coming from that plant runs all our electrical appliances and equipments in our houses each day. We do not see the current running to our refrigerators, television sets or computers. When all the equipments stop functioning, we realize the power has stopped. There are so many similar examples in our daily lives.

God gives existence to the thought and idea and places it before you. But He is so near that you cannot see Him with your eyes. That sounds so strange until the eyes of your heart are activated to spiritually feel His presence. Then you find Him so close.

Whatever you do, your intellect is with you, initiating the action. But you cannot see the intellect although you see its effects. Try to count things such as oxygen which you use every day but you are unable to physically see the presence of these things.

The heavens and the earth do not encompass God, but He encompasses the whole universe. His blessed Face is everywhere.

55

God Nourishes and Sustains all Creations

God provides sustenance to even a spider.

"And so many of moving (living) creatures are unable to carry their own provisions! God provides for them and for you. And He is the All-Hearing, the All-Knower."[133]

God is giving an example of a spider that she cannot carry her own sustenance but God provides for her as well as us human beings.

How difficult it is to work and feed yourself and your family. God arranges many meals per day for each of His billions of creations, both visible and invisible; He feeds them physically and spiritually. This task is beyond our imagination. He creates and arranges the food and inspires each creation on where and how to find this food and establishes the chain of never-ending supplies.

God sustains His creation. There is a physical sustenance and a spiritual sustenance. In the case of human beings, one should count as physical sustenance not only food, fruits, vegetables, milk, meats, drink, air, and clothing but also other gifts like knowledge and intelligence.

There is nothing empty or useless in the universe. Every single creation is a miracle, as is indicated in the verse:

"Our Lord, You have not created this universe in vain."[134]

All material sustenance is pure in origin. Only if it is soiled by the hand of man does it become undesirable, hateful and unlawful. Therefore man first has to seek and find the elements of sustenance in everything.

The spiritual sustenance is contained in the holy books. There might have been more scrolls from God in the ancient times. Just as one has to make efforts to gain material sustenance, one can receive spiritual sustenance from the holy books to a degree of their interest, passion, and research. If the person has positive intention, he will receive wisdom, but if a person has negative intention, the person can receive negative meaning and statements and interpretations to enforce his negative inclination. As is mentioned in the Quran many people have received guidance from it and many have misguided themselves through misinterpretation. It depends on one's intention and purity of the heart. Whether somebody believes or disbelieves, the Truth never changes. This does not affect God's honor, glory and majesty in any way.

If you attend a famous university with the intention of learning, you will become a scholar in your field of interest; however, if you attend the university with the intention of critiquing the educational system and the books, you can end up confused and with incomplete knowledge and views.

God nourishes all creation.

God creates nourishment for each of His creatures before He creates them. He creates the means for all creation to receive their nourishment according to their needs on a daily basis. Each organ in your body needs its own specific nourishment, and God ensures that they receive their nourishment.

He arranges for our spiritual nourishment according to the thirst of each seeker. He does not force anything on anyone. We have to seek spiritual nourishment just like we seek physical nourishment. He is protecting all creations through essential nourishment and energy.

He ensures the survival and growth of the body, mind, heart, and the soul and each elements of the body through the necessary dose of nourishment to generate the power and the energy.

56

God is the Best Teacher
and Guide

There is no compulsion in Surrender to Him, only persuasion.

Guidance is the wisdom you gain to lead your life, so that you can be successful in this world and the next world. There is no compulsion on any human being. He has given us freedom of choice. He guides those who show interest, intention, and initiative for guidance and surrender to Him

> *"We have created the way (of life); whoever wishes, can become thankful. Whoever wishes can be ungrateful."*[135]

God is the wise teacher to the path of love.

God uses even ants, spiders, bees, and stars to teach mankind through their examples. He is the most simple and wisest teacher who is available to all His creation day and night twenty-four/seven eternally.

He is ready to fill your heart with light. In His wisdom He leads all matters and affairs to their finality in a perfect way. He leads those interested to the straight path and salvation. He is a perfect teacher who never fails in His wisdom or in His actions and plans. Through His books, he has taught man bliss, prosperity and salvation. He has given us free will to learn and act on that learning. Although Almighty God is able to enforce His commands, He chooses to let man gain his rewards by his own choice and decision in acting on what he is taught.

The relationship with God enables man to become conscious of the truth and become disciplined. He knows how to use his intelligence and train his ego. He can learn the secrets of the divine and live his daily life in the best way.

God is the best teacher who can demonstrate how His will, power, and compassion work in the daily events, e.g. through His holy book. The seeker starts seeing and analyzing that certain event happened because of a specific action. He starts perceiving the cause and effect of the things happening all around because nothing happens on this earth without a reason. The wise seeker observes and reflects on the events taking place in the world. God sent great teachers like Abraham, Moses, Jesus, and Muhammad. He might have sent many other teachers in different parts of the world in ancient times. It would be appropriate to write about a few great prophets and teachers who are represented by billions of followers even to this day.

Abraham so Close to God Father of the Prophets
A One Man Nation Due to his Noble Character

Abraham was so close to God and loved Him intensely as expressed in his own words:

"For me, I have set my face, firmly and truly, towards God who

Created the Heavens and the earth, and never shall I associate partners in worship of God." [136]

God chose him to be the leader and a model to the nations as expressed in this verse:

"I shall make thee leader to the nations and a model" [137]

Abraham was indeed a prophet, a leader and a model to the future nations. A nation in himself, he was devoutly obedient to God, standing alone against his world. Due to his excellent character and firm belief, God calls him a one man nation. This is a unique honor from God for Abraham.

He was true in faith and he never joined other gods in worship to God. He had a pure and firm faith. Abraham showed his gratitude for the favors of God who chose him and guided him to a straight way. God gave him dignity in this world, and he will be, in the hereafter, in the ranks of the righteous in paradise and close to God

He approached his Lord with a sound heart which had the true love of God. A heart that is pure and unaffected by the negatives that afflict others, as the heart in spiritual terms is taken to be not only the seat of feelings and affections, but also of intelligence and resulting action. It implies the whole character.

God chose Abraham as a Friend

"Who can be better in religion than one who submits his whole self to God? Does well, and follows the way of Abraham the true in faith? For God did take Abraham for a Friend" [138]

His faith and conduct were firm and righteous in all circumstances. He was the fountainhead of the present monotheistic tradition, and is revered alike as the great Prophet of God by Jews Christians and Muslims.

He was God's messenger and he rejected worship of heavenly bodies and idols. He was willing to sacrifice anything for God even his own son whom he loved very much.

The Prophet Muhammad considered Abraham as his role model due to his excellent character. We can write volumes of book with the exemplary life of Abraham.

Moses - Before the Blessed Face of God

God Spoke to Moses directly

God spoke directly to Moses on Mt Sinai. This story can be found in the scriptures representing the three great religions of the world, i.e., Judaism, Christianity and Islam

"O Moses! Verily I am God, the Lord of the worlds." 139

There is a powerful message in the story of Moses as it shows God's presence and closeness to Moses and how Moses spoke to God directly:

Moses is loved and chosen by God and given his Mission

The spiritual history of Moses began when he received his mission. It was his spiritual birth. When Moses grew up, he left the palace of Pharaoh and went to the Midianite people in the Sinai Peninsula. He married a young lady from among them and was now travelling with his family and his flocks. He was called to his mission by God.

Moses saw a fire on the Mount Sinai and he said to his family that perhaps he can bring some burning brand or find some guidance at the fire. But it was not an ordinary fire. It was a Burning Bush: a Sign of the Glory of God and His Presence. But when Moses came to the fire, he heard a voice:

"Blessed are those close to the fire and those around; and Glory to God, the Lord of the Worlds"[140]

"O Moses! Verily I am thy Lord! Therefore (in my presence) take off thy shoes: you are in the sacred valley of Tuwa. I have chosen thee, Listen, then to the inspiration. Verily I am God: there is no god but I."

So serve you only Me and establish regular prayer for celebrating My

remembrance and praise." [141]

Moses received the famous ten Commandments. God gave him miracles and he was instructed to go to Pharaoh for Pharaoh had transgressed all bounds in oppressing and persecuting the Jewish people in bondage. Moses' brother, Aaron, was to be his deputy in this sacred mission. God reminded Moses how He loved him:

"But I cast (the garment of) **Love over thee from Me.**
And (this) in order that thou may be reared under Mine Eye (when he was young)"[142]

"And I have prepared thee for Myself (for mission)"Go, both of you to Pharaoh, for he has indeed transgressed all bounds." [143]

God informed Moses not to have any fear of Pharaoh "For I am with you; I Hear and See (everything)." The Universal Lord and Cherisher are the One and Only God, Who had created all beings and all things. It was from Him that each created thing derived its form and nature, including free will and power.

God forgives again and again those who repent, believe and do right. But Pharaoh was too arrogant to accept the message of Moses and he made a proclamation, saying, "I am your Lord, Most High." But God did punish him through drowning him and his army and left an example of him for the future generations. Moses organised his people to fight with the sword but was raised to God's mercy and his brother had to carry out Moses's mission.

Moses is remembered daily by billions of people due to his great character and courageous service to God. His story is full of lessons for generations to come.

In later history, David, though a mere shepherd boy, was chosen by God to lead his people. He overthrew the greatest warrior of his time, became a king and waged successful wars, being also a prophet, a poet and a musician. David used to sing and praise God and his love for God is preserved in the Psalms of David in the Old Testament.

Jesus: A Spirit from God and His Great Prophet

Jesus restores the life of a dead person and heals the sick

Jesus had no human father, as his birth was miraculous. It was not this which raised him to his high spiritual position as a great Prophet, but because God gave him a mission and supported him through the Holy Spirit (Gabriel) The miracles which surround his story relate not only to his birth, his life, and his being raised to heavens, but also to his mother Mary and his precursor the Prophet John. Jesus was a great spiritual leader, a teacher and a messenger from God.

All the scientists of the modern world can get together and with all the resources and billions of dollars at their disposal cannot restore a dead person back to life, the miracle performed by Jesus Christ by the power and permission of God.

Yet, when Jesus himself was persecuted and the Romans tried to kill him he did not have an army of followers to confront and remove the enemies from his way as was done by Prophet Moses when he was confronted by Pharaoh. Pharaoh and his army were all drowned in the Red Sea after Moses and his people safely crossed it.

Jesus was a Sign, a Spirit and a Mercy from God. Mary, his mother, was a virtuous and chaste woman who gave birth to Jesus through a miraculous virgin birth. God says:

Be, and it is!

"Mary said: "O my Lord! How shall I have a son when no man hath touched me? He said: "Even so: God creates What He wills: When He has decreed a plan, He says to it, 'Be,' and it is!"[144]

"We breathed into her of Our Spirit and We made her and her son a Sign and a Miracle for all future generations of people"[145]

"The son of Mary, held in Honor in this world and the Hereafter and will be among those brought Nearest to God."[146]

"And God will teach him (Jesus)
The Gospel, wisdom, law and (appoint him) His Messenger."[147]

Jesus tells people that "I make for you out of clay, as it were the figure of a bird, and breathe into it and it becomes a bird (alive) by God's permission and I heal those born blind, and the lepers, and I restore the life of the dead, by God's leave; and I declare to you what ye eat, and what ye store in your houses. Surely therein is a sign for you." He said "It is God who is my Lord and your Lord; Then worship Him, this is the Straight Way."[148]

"The similitude of Jesus before God is as that of Adam; He created Adam from dust, then said to him: "Be": And Jesus was created without a father." [149]

Jesus was born without a human father; But Adam was born without either a human father or mother. True wisdom consists in understanding the unity of the Divine purpose and the Unity of the Divine personality. Jesus came to teach the same message which God gave first to Abraham. Jesus came with the Gospel and the new laws

> *"We gave Moses the Book and followed him up with a succession of messengers; We gave Jesus, the son of Mary, clear signs (Gospel) and strengthened him with the Holy Spirit."*[150]

As an infant, Jesus Spoke to People miraculously

When Jesus was a baby and people were accusing Mary of adultery and a child out of wedlock, she pointed to the baby that they can ask him (Jesus). They said:

"How can we talk to one who is an infant in the cradle?

He (Jesus) said: I am indeed a servant of God;

He (God) has given me Scripture and made me a Prophet;

And He has made me blessed wherever I maybe, and has enjoined on me prayer and charity as long as I live. He has made me kind to my

Mother, and not overbearing or miserable."[151]

Jesus said: "Peace be on me the day I am born, the day I die, and the day I am raised."

"So Peace is on me the day I was born, the day that I die, and the Day that I shall be raised up to life. Such was Jesus the son of Mary (it is) a statement of the truth,"[152]

Then will God say:"Jesus son of Mary! Recount My favor to you and to your mother, Behold! I strengthened you with the Holy

Spirit so that you speak to the people in the cradle and in maturity.

Behold! I taught thee the Book, the wisdom, the law, and the Gospel.

Behold! You make out of clay, as it were the figure of a bird, by My

Leave, and you breathe into it, and it becomes an alive bird by My leave, and you heal those born blind, and the lepers by My leave and you bring forth the dead by My Leave."[153]

Miracle of the Last Super

Said Jesus: O' God our Lord! Send us from heaven a table set that there may be for us for the first and the last of us a solemn festival and a Sign from Thee; and provide for our sustenance, for Thou art the best Sustainers (of all our needs)"
154

The last super was arranged by God through angels providing all kinds of foods according to the wish of Jesus.

Muhammad – the last Messenger of God

God called him 'Mercy to all the Worlds.'

The Prophet Muhammad was born in Arabia about 500 years after the mission of Jesus Christ. Muhammad was an orphan as his father Abdullah died young before the child was born, leaving no property. His mother Aminah was in ailing health and he was looked after by his nurse Halimah. His mother herself died when he was only six years old and his aged grandfather Abdul Muttalib took care of him but he too passed away two years later. Then his uncle Abu Talib took care of him.

The Prophet Muhammad joined caravans carrying merchandise to Syria on behalf of a wealthy trading lady named Khadija who was a widow. She was so much impressed by the honesty and trading skills of the Prophet Muhammad that she sent her sister with a marriage proposal to him. The Prophet Muhammad accepted it and set a model by marrying a widow 15 years his senior. She gave birth to all their children during their successful married life of 26 years. He had her as his only wife for 26 years.

Due to his great character, the Prophet Muhammad was recognized as the truthful and trustworthy even by the pagans of Mecca. The pagans in Arabia worshipped hundreds of idols, stones, stars and the moon. The idolatry of his people, immorality and oppression of women and slaves set the Prophet Muhammad's mind and soul aflame. He would often retire to the solitude of a high mountain called the mountain of light and in a cave named Hira outside Mecca for contemplation. When he turned forty years of age, the arch angel Gabriel appeared to the Prophet Muhammad in the cave saying God had chosen him as His last messenger to convey the message of Oneness of God.

He went through more suffering in his life than any other Prophet

God loved him dearly and he was God's beloved. The Prophet announced to his people that there is no deity to be worshipped except God and that he is the last Messenger from Him. Thus continuing the chain of previous prophets like Abraham, Moses and Jesus. He informed them to surrender to God instead of hundreds of idol gods they used to worship. He was subjected to persecution and oppression but his faith was never shaken. The Prophet Muhammad lost his noble uncle and protector, Abu Talib, and then his beloved wife Khadija in whose devotion and companionship he had found comfort and solace during the days of the people's denial of him and his persecution.

Finally, the pagans selected forty strong tribal men offering them reward for killing the Prophet Muhammad who migrated to the city of Medina about 200 miles away. This event is called the Hijra or migration of the Prophet and is the starting point of the Islamic calendar. The pagans still continued pursuing him until finally God gave permission to the Prophet to defend himself. The pagans organized three invasions against the Prophet but all were beaten back with huge losses to the pagans. The Prophet Muhammad lost scores of friends and was himself severely wounded.

Go people, you all are free today

After years of struggle, patience and sacrifice, the Prophet Muhammad wanted to avoid bloodshed at any cost and, through God's grace, he was able to achieve a peaceful victory over the pagans of Mecca. He finally entered the city of Mecca and destroyed hundreds of idol gods. If the Prophet Muhammad were a violent man, he would have taken revenge of his persecution and killing of his beloved uncle, relatives and followers. "Go, you all are free!" were the words in which the Prophet Muhammad gave the pagans general amnesty. Thousands of pagan enemies were so much impressed by the kindness and forgiveness of the Prophet that they started embracing Islam. The Prophet is God's beloved and mercy to all the worlds.

After his annual pilgrimage to Mecca, the Prophet Muhammad received the revelation from God that the religion had now been completed and preserved in the Quran and he had accomplished his mission as people were entering Islam in thousands. On his return to Medina, he fell ill of a mortal fever. It is reported that the angel Gabriel brought a message to the Prophet that he had a choice of living as long as he wished or returning to his Lord God. He chose to return to God whom he had loved intensely all his life. His fever lasted for fifteen days and he passed away praying for the guidance of all mankind. He deputized, Abu Bakr, his closest friend and supporter from the first day of his mission.

Under the Prophet's leadership, scores of his companions had received high spiritual knowledge and training to lead the nation, notably Abu Bakr, Omar, Uthman, Ali and many more. The

Prophet's daughter Fatima was one of the most righteous young ladies. She was married to Ali and was very devoted to him. Their sons Hassan and Hossain were the apples of the Prophet's eyes. These two brave young men played significant role in the nation's affairs. The Prophet's widow Aiysha, called the mother of the believers, family and companions continued spreading his teachings after him.

The Prophet Muhammad did not claim to be the founder of a new religion. His mission was to purify and restore the earlier messages of Abraham, Moses and Jesus and the Quran confirms the earlier scriptures of the Torah and Bible. There is neither monasticism nor priesthood in Islam which is based on compassion and tolerance towards all human beings and love of God. Due to politically motivated violent actions, some muslim groups have given Islam a negative image. When Jewish people were being persecuted in Europe about 800 years ago, the Muslim rulers of Spain welcomed them to settle and enjoy the freedom in Spain. They received all the protection and flourished in Spain.

The Prophet Muhammad lived in great humility and was never the first to withdraw his hand from a handshake and never passed a group of children playing without a smile and kind words to them.

Thousands of non-muslim writers have paid tributes to the wisdom and character of the Prophet Muhammad including the famous writers Napoleon Hill, Michael Heart, Sir George Bernard Shaw, Thomas Carlyle and Ghandi.

He outlawed the practice of slavery and provided laws for a successful marriage and family life. He showed by his own example that men should treat women with respect and dignity. He freed slave men, women and young girls and took care of the orphans, poor and homeless. After fourteen hundreds years, there are now sixty Muslim countries and the Muslim population is estimated at 1.7 billions.

> The Quran clearly shows tolerance towards all people, belief in God and in His messengers: "You say: We believe in God, and the revelation given to us, and to Abraham, Ishmail, Isaac, Jacob, and the tribes, and that given to Moses and Jesus, and that given to (all) Prophets from their Lord. We make no difference between one and another of them and we surrender to God"[155]

"And dispute ye not with the people of the Book except in the best way

> It be with those of them who inflict wrong (and injury) but say, "We believe in the revelation which has come down to us and in that which came down to you; our God and your God is One; and it is to Him we surrender." [156]

Don't be an aggressor, make Peace God loves not the aggressors.

Don't be an aggressor, make peace: Islam is against all kinds of aggression; sanction is given for war only in self-defence. 'Fight in the way of God against those who attack you, but begin not hostilities. Verily God loves not the aggressors. And if they (your enemy) incline towards peace, incline thou also to it, and trust in God." [157]

There is no compulsion in Islam. You can invite people but not force anyone. The rights of God, family, relatives, neighbors and mankind are clearly shown. The Prophet always put his trust in God and unto Him he looked for help and guidance. "The prophet does not talk except what is inspired to him by God." [158]

As the Sun spreading light: O Prophet! Truly we have sent thee as a Witness, Bearer of Glad tidings, and a Warner and as one who invites to God by His leave, and as a sun (a spiritual sun spreading light to illuminate the whole world. When the sun appears all the lesser lights pale before its light)." [159]

"Now wait in patience for the Command of thy Lord: For verily thou art in our eyes: And celebrate the praises of thy Lord while you stand firmly in prayer (during the night)." [160]

Excellent Character. 'You have indeed in the Messenger of God a beautiful model for any one whose hope is in God and the final day and who engages much in the remembrance of God." [161]

The Prophet's virtues, the excellent character, and his love for mankind were fully recognised in his lifetime and his name stands highest among the heroic leaders of mankind.

Mercy. "We sent thee not, but as a Mercy for all creations."[162]

The extremely gentle nature of Muhammad endeared him to all and God named him as "Mercy to all Creation." It is a God-like quality, which binds the souls of countless men to him. The tender heart of the teacher is grieved that anyone should suffer in any way.

"Have We not expanded thee thy breast?"[163]

The Prophet's human nature had been purified, expanded and elevated to a higher level of excellence and patience.

Marriage. The Prophet had one wife Khadija for the 26 years of his adult life. In the later years of his life, some widows got married to him to seek security, support and tribal unity. Also, he got married to young Aiysha who, due to being young, passed knowledge about his personal life to next generations, as to how a husband should treat his wife with love and care. Muslims have the lowest marriage failures and have firm family life.

> *"Stand (in prayer) part of the night, but not all night. That your God is One God: whoever expects to meet his Lord let him work righteousness and in the worship of his Lord, admit no one as partner."* [164]

> *Justice. God is never unjust in the least degree; if there is any good He doubles it, and gives from His own Presence a great reward."*[165]

The Orphan. He treated all orphans with tender care, affection and respect as he was an orphan himself.

Women dignified

Quran honors and dignifies women by mentioning examples of virtuous Maryam, wives of Abraham and Asia wife of Pharaoh. Men and women have different duties, functions and responsibilities. Through devotion, women can get even closer to God than men. As it happened with Rabiah Basri in Iraq about 1200 year ago, she was a muslim saintly woman and many famous men scholars used to visit her to learn spiritual knowledge and love of God. Her inspiring quotes can be found in the books to this day.

"Recite what is sent of the Book by inspiration to thee, and establish regular prayer: for prayer restrains one from evil and unjust deeds; and remembrance of God is the greatest (virtue) without doubt and God knows (actions) what ye do."[166]

Some quotes of the Prophet Muhammad

Do you love your Creator? Then love your fellow human being too.

Keep smiling as: to smile is a charity.

The true wealth is the good you do in this world

It is your own conduct which will lead you to reward or punishment, as if you had been destined thereof.

People have suffering in their lives due to the result of what they say with their tongues.

Riches are not from an abundance of worldly goods but from a contented heart.

God enjoins you to treat women well, for they are your mothers, daughters, sisters and wives.

Those who are patient in adversity and forgive wrongs are the doers of excellence

Say what is true, although it may be bitter and displeasing to people

The most excellent struggle is that for the conquest of the self.

If you show mercy to those who are in the earth, He Who is in the heaven will show mercy to you.

What is faith? When your good deed pleases you and your evil deed grieves you, you are a believer. What is sin? When a thing disturbs (the peace of) your heart, give it up.

Prophet Muhammad was the perfect example of a human being due to his excellent character.

Mary: One of the Great Women Leaders of all time

Mary, the mother of Jesus Christ was a woman of highest virtue and character. She was placed in one of the greatest trial a woman can go through. She was chosen to be the mother of Jesus who was supposed to be born of virgin birth which had never happened before. People could not understand this miracle and started accusing her of adultery. She went into privacy from her people for prayer and devotion to God.

It was in the state of purity that the angel appeared to her in the shape of a man. Chastity was the special virtue of Mary: with a son of virgin birth, she and Jesus became a great miracle to all nations. The angel came in the shape of a man and announced to her the good news of a son whose name will be Jesus Christ, a spirit and a word from God. He will be held in Honor in this world and the Hereafter and will be of those nearest to God. Further, he shall speak to the people in childhood and in maturity.

> *"Relate in the Book of Mary, when she withdrew from her family to a place in the East. God had destined her to be the mother of the Prophet Jesus Christ." She placed a screen from them; Then We sent to her Our angel, and he appeared before her as a man in all respects. She said "I seek refuge from thee to (God) Most Gracious (come not near) if you do fear God."*
> 167

> *"He said: "Nay, I am only a messenger from thy Lord, (to announce) to thee the gift of a holy son. She said: How shall*

I have a son, seeing that no man has touched me, and I am not unchaste." [168]

God creates What He Wills. When He decrees a Plan, He says to it, 'Be,' and it is! He said: "So (it will be); Thy Lord says: That is easy for Me: and We wish to appoint him as a Sign unto men and a mercy from Us. It is a matter already decreed." [169]

"So she conceived him (through a miracle) and she retired with him to a remote place. And the pains of childbirth drove her to the trunk of a palm tree. She cried (in her anguish): "Ah! Would that I had died before this! Would that I had been a thing forgotten and out of sight." [170]

"But (a voice) cried to her from beneath the (palm tree): "Grieve not! For thy Lord has provided a spring beneath thee; and shake towards thyself the trunk of the palm tree; it will let fall fresh ripe dates upon thee. So eat, and drink and cool (thine) eyes." [171]

*"And (remember) her who guarded her chastity; We breathed into her of **Our Spirit,** and We made her and her son a Sign (miracle) for all mankind."* [172]

Mary was elevated to a higher place in paradise

Jesus loved his mother Mary. She was elevated to a higher place in paradise and became a model for women for future generations.

Rumi, One of the great spiritual teachers and lover of God

Jalal-ud-Din Rumi is one of the great spiritual teachers on the Path of Love. He lived in the twelveth century in the Turkish city of Konya. He is considered one of the great spiritual poets in the East and his poetry has been translated in all major languages. His message of love is universal and his poetry has been appreciated by people of all religions. As a teacher, he guided his students on the way of self-purification and spiritual perfection. His poetry shows a simple way of connecting directly with the Divine.

Rumi was an acknowledged scholar in the jurisprudence (the science of the Shari'ah, Arabic grammar, the Quran, Hadith, Quranic commentary, history, dogmatics, theology, logic, philosophy, mathematics and astronomy. His name is listed among the lists of the doctors of the Law belonging to the Hanafi school.

Rumi had traversed the stations of the spiritual path of love and realized the direct and immediate vision of God he discusses so often in his poetry. He has explained the love and wisdom of this path through poetry and short stories. Due to the large circulation of his poetry books, he is considered as one of the most popular poets in America.

Mother Rabiah teacher to the path of God's light and love

Many years ago, I had a dream in which I saw the verse "God is the Light of the heavens and the earth" written across the sky above from the east to the west. In the dream, it was night time and the verse was written in the sky with the glittering and shining light. I was gazing at this wonderful illuminated message on the sky above. At that time, a very spiritual lady called mother Rabiah who was my spiritual teacher explained to me that the dream has a clear message. The loving Creator was showing me that my spiritual path in life is the path of love and light which was her path too. Through her guidance, I was able to advance spiritually

She became a widow with children while still very young. This tragedy turned her to the spiritual path of love of God. She started teaching the love of God to thousands of young girls, women and a few young men. People used to give her gifts of money which she would give to the sick and poor families. She never kept any money or gifts. I had seen so many practical miracles of her. My mother, who had a very soft heart, was also her student. The teacher used to fast frequently. She had an amazing power of faith and was still spiritually conscious when she was close to 100 years of age.

I have never seen a spiritually more powerful woman than this teacher. She turned her house into a spiritual center where she provided guidance to her students. I saw her large house, in a dream, as a garden in paradise. She had completed her mission and passed away when she was over one hundred years of age. Even after passing away, she came to teach me a few times in dream. Once in a dream, we were waiting for the Prophet Muhammad to visit our house. All of sudden, the house got illuminated with light as it was night time. The Prophet was standing a few feet away and smiling. My teacher told me to go and greet the Prophet. I stepped forward to greet and meet the Prophet face to face (I have never seen a more beautiful face). Later on, I was also blessed with meeting, in dreams, the great Prophets Jesus and Moses.

I learnt very deep inner spiritual meanings of the verses of the Quran and the traditions from another spiritual teacher named Malik Mohammad Abdullah. He was an engineer by background but also was the follower of the path of love. He had Quranic knowledge of the spiritual interpretations of dreams which I learnt from him. He was close to God and used to have many spiritual experiences. The Prophet Joseph had been given special spiritual knowledge by God for the dreams interpretations.

The great spiritual teacher in the Path of Ishq - Love

A few years later, God opened the way for me to meet another great spiritual teacher Baba Gulzar Ahmed Sabri whom I have found to be the highest in the Ishq or love of God. I consider this teacher to be the most spiritually advanced and closer to God than anyone in the world. He experiences the presence of God within.

He has an excellent character and he told me that he does not forget God even for a second due to his intense love for Him. He said God is always with him as He loves him too. I don't have his permission to write more things about him as he doesn't like to make a show. He says it is God Himself who cures and does miracles and he should not get credit which he said belongs only to God.

His mission is to spread love and spiritually connect people to God. He teaches spiritual knowledge which is not commonly found in the books. He has thousands of students all over the world.

57

The Soul or the Spirit is from God

Your invisible Soul Sees God

"They will ask you about the soul (spirit). Say: The soul or spirit is from the Command of my Lord...."[173]

God is the Creator and beloved of the soul.

God is the focus of the soul because He created it. It longs passionately for the infinite beauty. When one is aware of one's soul, then the senses follow the soul.

The soul of a person and the creator of that soul are eternal.

When God loves His servant, He instills in him consciousness and realization of the soul, which is nothing less than a miracle. The human body is the outward manifestation of the spirit or soul.

God transcends all souls. Man's soul is greater than the animal soul as the human soul has more awareness. The angel's soul is greater than human soul, as it transcends the rational senses. When the seeker of the blessed Face achieves closeness to God, his soul becomes even greater than that of the angel's. God commanded the angels to prostrate themselves before Adam because God had instilled him with His attributes and qualities. This prostration symbolizes angels being in service to mankind. Rumi says:

The soul is one-half of a leaf from the garden of Thy Beauty

Open your eyes! See the spirits that have fled from the body!
The spirit has smashed the cage; the heart has fled from the body!
What is the spirit? One-half of a leaf from the garden of Thy Beauty.
What is the heart? A single blossom from Thy provisions and plenty.
Without doubt the intellects and hearts derive from the Divine Throne, but they live veiled from the Throne's Light.

Your invisible soul sees God but you are unaware of it

The body is outward, but the spirit or soul is hidden; the body is like the sleeve, and the soul the hand. Then intellect is more hidden than soul and the senses perceive the spirit more quickly than the body.

You see a movement and you know there is life. But you do not know if it is filled with intellect. The soul of prophetic revelation is beyond the intellect; coming from the unseen, it belongs to that side.

He takes your soul by night

"It is He who takes your souls by night (when you are asleep), and has knowledge of all that you have done by day, and then He raises (awakens) you up again that a term appointed (your life period) be fulfilled, then (in the end) unto Him will be your return. He will then inform you of that which you used to do."[174]

We know that all creation is subject to His laws and plans, as is man's life in every aspect and at every moment, awake or asleep. The mystery of sleep, "the twin brother of death," is called the taking of our soul by Him. The record of all we have done in our waking moments remains with us and glimpses of this record sometimes appears to us in dreams.

By day we awaken again to our daily activities and this process goes on in our entire life until we fulfill the term of our lives appointed for us on this earth. Then comes the other sleep with the full record of our lives. In the end, we face the final reality of resurrection and judgment, at which time we see everything clearly and not as seen in dreams. The spiritual people can experience future events to come while still in this world and will not be surprised. The other people who are unaware will be in a great shock and awe to see the events of the next world.

The soul in the body is like a battery in a car.

Soul is like a battery in the car. You can buy the most expensive car but it will not start and run unless it has a good battery. The battery helps the engine to start and run. Then the car starts moving. The soul is like a spiritual battery in the human body. Just as a car would not start or move without a charged battery, the body cannot function without the soul. When it leaves, the body becomes motionless. When the soul is in joy, the person feels permanent bliss.

When the soul is fine, all parts of the body like the brain, heart and lungs function properly. If the soul is weak and depressed, the entire body is adversely affected.

Remembrance of God and contemplation keeps the soul charged

Spiritual path keeps the soul in excellent condition. Remembrance of God, contemplation and good deeds keep the soul charged and happy.

58

Great Universe Hidden within Man

"I was a hidden treasure and I wished to be known so I Created the universe."[175]

There are quantum efforts being focused on discovering more of the universe, but there is hardly any interest or effort to discover the great universe and mysteries hidden within man.

That is why God invites mankind to reflect by saying:

"Why don't they reflect in their own selves?"[176]

While we are all busy in the race to acquire material wealth, we could take some time off and think of the treasure hidden within us. After all, the great innovations in technology, tall buildings, long bridges, planes, trains, ships, factories and scientific advances in medicine and other areas have come from the mind of man. These inventions resulted from the silent efforts, focus, and tireless research and ideas developed by men and women.

Similarly, we could spare some time and devote a few moments in silence and in contemplation of our own creation and reflect deep in our hearts to find peace and contentment. Through further focus and striving, we could discover the light and the presence of the loving Creator God who has promised that:

"Whoever strives in Us, the way will be opened for him." [177]

The priorities in life keep everyone busy. Many people with the highest education and achievements are unable to understand and appreciate and thus remain ignorant of the hidden realities and mysteries of life. They could try to discover the universe hidden within them.

The Hidden Treasure within man.

All those who spent their lifetime discovering the universe hidden within have never received a Noble Prize or world applause because the treasure they discover is that which can never be matched in value or honor if the entire world and everything in it were to be a prize.

People have developed instruments and equipment and have been able to discover the hidden oil wells deep in the earth and even oceans. They received huge material rewards for this marvelous work. What about the hidden universe within us?

You can see the presence of the sun, moon and stars in the world.

God challenges mankind to come close to Him and discover His presence everywhere. You can see the presence of the sun, moon and stars from any part of the world. Those who strived and persevered to develop longing for God in their hearts and minds were able to discover the presence of the blessed Face of God everywhere.

59

Remove Veils to Show Your Perfect Beauty

Discover the beauty of the true Beloved.

Remove your veil, so that we may see your incredible beauty, You, the Beloved of visible and invisible creations in the universe.

Every other object of love veils His Face.

The seekers contemplate God's image of beauty in their hearts. The divine attributes of beauty, mercy, gentleness, compassion, generosity and kindness reflect true beauty in the material world.

Good and evil, joy and sorrow, and blessing and tribulation are all real and are the outcome or varying appearances of the Divine attributes.

In the words of great Rumi:

Fly to the unseen! Go to the hidden house, Oh my thought and comprehension! God's Beauty is the object and worthy of our love.

The temporal cannot know the Eternal, to the extent that the seeker contemplates God in his heart, God Himself is the contemplator.

Since God is the only permanent existence, ultimately when the seeker is in the depth of contemplation, he feels like the Witness, the Witnessed, and the Witnessing are all One. In the spiritual language, this state is called annihilation. Witness within the heart is the seeker, who has been transformed into a locus of manifestation of God's Beauty and has become His beloved.

Manifestation of God's Beauty and His Blessed Face

When the corner of your heart becomes a house of worship, love, and a polished mirror, it reflects the perfection and majesty of God.

I will place this shattered heart before **Thy Face,**
If it should speak of faithfulness, I will say, "Is this faithfulness?"
In the everlasting Presence, you are the Witness and the Witnessed!
You laugh at the Path, the traveler, migration, and journeying!
You have lifted up your head between annihilation and obliteration.

Behold the worshipers of God's Command, drowned in His Command, with their divine gifts, their beauty, and their witness-nature. Muhammad is the intercessor for every disgrace because his eye did not swerve from God.

In the night – this world – where the Sun is veiled, He kept his vision on God and had hope in Him.

His eyes received special light from God:

> *"Did we not expand thy breast (with light)?"* [178]

He beheld what Gabriel could not bear...He contemplated the stations of all God's servants; hence God named him the "Witness"

The tools of the Witness are a tongue and eyes so keen that no secret can elude his nightly vigil. God wants you to become pious, so that you will leave aside self-interest and become a witness. For these self-interested motives are veils upon the eyes, twisted around the vision like blindfolds...

God possesses nothing in the lofty heavens and in the earth more precious than man's soul.

So, since the Prophet's mighty eyes saw that spirit, nothing remained hidden from him.

In the two worlds God gazes on the heart, as a king gazes on the servant.

God's love and the mystery of His "contemplation of the witness" are the foundation of His entire veil making. Therefore our contemplator of the witness said:

"But for thee" at the time of the encounter on the night of the acsension (Mairaj)."

Joy to you, oh keen-sighted Prophet pleasing to God! Next to the shore of my spirit's sea, the ocean is less than a drop. The beautiful and ravishing beloved represents appearance of His gentleness!

60

The Ego and the Intellect

When patience and intellect go, your ego inclines to evil.

There are two kinds of intellect: universal and partial.

The universal intellect is sufficient and has no need for any outside help. God bestows it, and its fountainhead lies in the midst of the spirit. The partial intellect needs nourishment from outside through learning and contemplation. You learn it through school, from books, teachers, reflection, and learning concepts and new sciences. Through gaining knowledge, your intellect becomes greater than that of others.

Seek the fountain within yourself.

Partial intellect has passion for the world and has deprived man of the object of his desire. The Prophet Muhammad was said to be unlettered not because he was incapable of writing or ignorant of the sciences, but because his writing, science, and wisdom were innate and not acquired. What was there in the world that he did not know? He was the institution of knowledge and wisdom, and everyone learned from him. What sort of thing could the partial intellect possess that is not possessed by the universal intellect?

The partial intellect is in need of teaching. But the universal intellect is the teacher, and it has no needs. The philosopher is in bondage to intellectual concepts; the pure seeker receives intellect from the universal intellect.

61

Know Thyself

Man is the universe in microcosm; the supreme creation.

"Why do they not reflect in their own selves..."[179]

"He, who knows his self, knows his Lord."[180]

The Science of the Self
The self is an invisible component of every human being.

The self is also called ego, which is used in a negative sense. Human inner self is inclined towards greed, but if he does well and keeps away from evil, God is well acquainted with what he does. The lowest self is the rebellious self, which can be turned into a contented self through training, molding, patience, and discipline.

Knowledge of Self

If you could but **know thyself** as you should,
You wilt gain the knowledge of the Universe
If you should care to know the Truth
Know thyself, not through speculation
But through illumination, search and faith
Be your own knower, for this is the way to know the Truth
You have turned into a philosopher but you know not
Where you are?
From where you have come?
And what you are?
O, Ignoramus!

Rumi

There are four major types of Selves.

There are four types of selves according to the Quran: the uncontrollable self, the partially controlled self, the contented self, and the sacrificed self.

The Basic Uncontrolable Self

The basic or uncontrollable self (ammara) is like an uncontrollable horse. The person is a kind of rebel and does not have respect for any human beings or any kind of decency. The person could be a king, a leader or an ordinary man. An extreme case of uncontrolled self can be found where one person's decision caused the deaths of millions of people.

This person acts according to whatever his self would dictate to him regardless of the consequences. Most of the problems in the world in the past and today are due to the people with uncontrollable selves. Unfortunately they represent the great majority of people. There is total absence of self-control in this type of self. They will cause destruction in the name of religion, justice, politics, honor, glory, pride, fame, family tradition, and so forth. People can choose a leader who has an uncontrolled self and whose decisions can bring suffering to millions of people including those who chose him in the first place. Many such people are not necessarily in low jobs or places, but many are in high authority and positions of power. They could be generals and even leaders of countries or religious organizations. A spiritual leader will never cause any suffering to any human being and can solve problems through wisdom, faith and without resorting to the oppressive force.

In the majority of cases, the society, old traditions, and the culture serve as the springboards for these people. If they are instructed, advised, and trained, they can become very honorable and respectful human beings. Many such people have been able to improve themselves.

You can see people who had no self-control but later became conscious of their weaknesses and improved their selves through character building and gained respect and honor.

The most effective way to discipline the self is through spirituality

The most effective way to discipline the self is through spirituality as detailed in this book. When you see celebrities spend millions of dollars on their weddings only to divorce in a matter of a few years, you're observing the uncontrolled self at work. These marriages and families could be saved through consultation with the spiritual teachers. The arguments, anger, accusations, and sometimes even violence and police, attorneys, and courts become part of the news because of the rage generated by the uncontrollable self. Life can dramatically improve and become so peaceful when the uncontrollable self has been improved.

The Partially Controlled Self

The partially controlled self (lawwama) exercises self-control but loses it at times. When the person does something wrong; upon realization, he becomes repentant and remorseful. This type of self engages in self-analysis and looks at consequences before initiating any destruction or damaging act. There are some people in the initial state or higher state of the partially controlled self.

The Contented Self

The contented self (mutma'inna) is a controlled, disciplined and restrained self. This person develops complete self-control through fasting, prayer, meditation and through guidance from

God. In this kind of self, the person can experience a state of living in paradise while still living in this world. This person feels so contented in his or her daily life that leaving this world for the next does not make any difference in terms of his or her state of mind and heart. It is paradise here and paradise in the next world. He or she enjoys presence of God.

He has tasted the joy of God's pleasure and as a result, feels total contentment and satisfaction right here, regardless of riches or poverty, big house or a small hut, big name in the society or unknown to people. He is happy with whatever comes his way. The person with contented self experiences closeness to God.

This person experiences the presence of the blessed Face of God.

The truly contented self can hear God honoring and addressing it:

> "O' you contented self, come and join this group of My special servants and all of you enter My paradise."[181]

This self shows you what is of great significance in this life and what is least important so that the person does not invest his life time chasing a dream which turns out to be like a mirage. As the thirsty person in a desert sees a water spring which, at close range, turns out to be a heap of sand. The person becomes conscious of reality and the truth.

The sacrificed Self

This person has truly realized the full potential of his or her life in all aspects of life. The person can find himself or herself sitting not too far from where the truly great ones are.

The sacrificed self is the highest noble state in which the person carries his life and property to be sacrificed at the wish and pleasure of the beloved God. This person does not cause harm to innocent people or act in a destructive manner. He does not feel ownership of anything not even his own self. He only sees God. He speaks and does what God inspires him to. He lives for God every moment and dies for God.

He lives like he is in the blessed hand of God each moment.

He donates to the poor and needy whatever he receives or earns. He would starve himself and feed others if necessary. He would not keep anything till tomorrow if there are people in need today. That does not mean that the person will become a monk. The person will live and get married and have children but place his wishes and desires in the hands of God. He would do what is legal in the sight of God and does not make his own rules to exploit people in the name of land, property, government, politics, or religion.

His sole purpose in life is listening to and serving God and serving human beings. He loves and is focused on his Beloved Creator and can sacrifice whatsoever the Beloved wishes, including his own life.

When this self is overpowered by difficulties, calamities, and distress, it turns toward God Almighty, establishes a connection with Him and severs all desires and lusts. This self knows what God wants from him.

God says about this type of self:

**I become his hearing, with which he hears,
I become his eyes, with which he sees,
I become his hands with which he strikes or works and
I become his feet with which he walks......
and in one tradition...I become his tongue with which
he speaks.** [182]

Then God speaks through him and acts through him. This ultimate state of self is expressed in the Prophet Muhammad where in the Quran God is instructing him to say:

"My prayer, my sacrifice, my life and my death are only for God, Lord of the entire universe" [183]

He feels nothing belongs to him and he lives every moment for God. All his actions are for pleasing God. In this case, the first goal, second, third, and the final are all God. There is nothing else in his life except the love of God.

"Now await in patience the command of thy Lord: for verily you are before Our Sight"[184]

God says that your companion the Prophet Muhammad does not speak to you of his own desire but speaks only when he receives revelation and inspiration from Him. Otherwise, he maintains silence and focused on whom He loves, God. At times when the Prophet was asked questions, he remained silent. Then the answer came to him from God and he would announce.

> *Once an angry lady came to the Prophet and disputed about a cultural practice which amounted to injustice towards women by men at that time. The Prophet kept silent while the lady was demanding that this practice which exploited women, should be banned immediately. Shortly after revelation came: God saying:"He heard the complaint of this lady and you are maintaining silence but God has heard it and from now on this practice is unlawful in favor of the lady. The chapter has been named 'the Dispute."[185]*

The great Rumi was willing to sacrifice anything to please his Beloved. He says that there is nothing more effective for character forming than the grief; the heart is purified and the self is polished. If you succeed in treating your cardiac diseases by means of grief and distress and attain to the state of patience or perseverance, grief has aided you in achieving the greatest victory and such a grief is better than a thousand joys – the joys on account of which you were a slave to lustfulness and were enveloped in darkness and were far from light. You had no contact with the God Almighty; the evil one had complete hold over you.

Umar, the Prophet's close companion, once said:

"I found superlative luxury in patience!"

When Abu Bakr Siddique, the truthful and closest companion of the Prophet fell ill people inquired of his health and asked whether they might send for a physician. He replied that the Physician had examined him. They asked him what the Physician said and he answered that the Physician (God) told him

"He did what He pleased"

The spiritual teacher Maruf Karkhi would often say, "That person is not a faithful servant who does not enjoy the lash of his Master (God) and his claims of being honest are false!"

God elevates you to higher ranks sometimes through adversity

Adversity is a tool for spiritual training

A person with this type of self knows that God Almighty is aware of his affliction and is witnessing it! God elevates you through tribulation to strengthen you and mold your character to excellence.

The Prophet Muhammad said that he has gone through more suffering and persecution in his life than all the sufferings that the other prophets of God went through.

"When God loves a person, sometimes He involves him in tribulation; if he bears it with patience, He makes him His elected one, and if he reconciles himself to Him, He exalts him to the highest rank" [186]

62

The Knowledge of God Himself

"The Knowledge is Light which God causes to descend into the hearts of whosoever He wishes."[187]

The knowledge of the essence of God is the key and one must believe in God's existence and realization that there is nothing like Him. He is eternal in His will and free from changes, without form, shape and beyond space. He is without any partner. Works and actions are created, willed, and fixed and changed by God. He is kind to creatures and doesn't impose anything on man that is beyond his limits. He does what He wills. When He loves you, He fulfills your wishes even before you ask.

Man keeps ignoring his soul's craving for God

God is the object of man's vision in this world. Man's soul is craving for God with every breath but man keeps ignoring his own soul. Man becomes focused to fulfill his desires and spends his life in the pursuit of material goals while his soul remains thirsty.

God invites mankind to strive and seek knowledge of Him

The first light that illumines faith and the first thing to be followed is the word of God and there is no word better than the Holy Scriptures:

> *"And those who strive in Us, We will certainly guide them to Our path. For verily, God is with those who strive for excellence."[188]*

God has promised that those who strive in His straight path through worshiping, fasting, and giving charity will be rewarded immensely. But in the above-mentioned verse, God is emphasizing that whoever strives in Him, the way will be opened for the seeker. Striving in His path is different from striving in Him as it means striving to love God and knowing His Essence, attributes and actions.

God invites mankind to know, love and achieve closeness to Him.

God has thousands of attributes, qualities and names. There are God's attributes in the Torah, in the Bible and in the Quran. Thousands of attributes have been summarized into ninety-nine attributes by the Prophet Muhammad who advised his companions to reflect on these attributes. These attributes represent knowledge of God and this knowledge leads to Paradise.

Ali, the Prophet's cousin and one of his closest companions, had an excellent character and a high spiritual rank. He said that his knowledge of God was so profound that if, per chance, God were to come physically in front of him that would not increase his knowledge of God any more than he had already acquired. He knew Him so well as if he were seeing Him.

> First come the knowledge of God Himself and then spiritual realization or the ascending stages of human perfection that results in closeness to God. The Prophet said: "The law is my words, the Way is my works, and the Truth is my inward state."[189]

Law is the rules. The way or Tariqah is then practice and dealings. The reality or Haqiqah is the inward state and stations attained by the seeker in his journey to God.

The law is like a lamp. The truth is attaining closeness to God.

Knowledge of God, man and the world derive ultimately from God. The seeker's way is to follow the model provided by the Prophet and the spiritual teachers who have advanced in this path through patience, love, striving and achieving closeness to God.

The love and knowledge of God can take away all fears

One man approached the great spiritual teacher Bayazid Bustami, who lived about 1150 years ago in Baghdad requesting the teacher if he could help him know God and get close to Him. Bayazid asked the man, as a first step, if he could go and spend a night in the cave on a nearby mountain. The man said that was easy. The next day that man came running back and asked Bayazid not to play with him as there was a huge monster snake in the cave and he had to run for his life. Bayazid said that if you have so much fear of just one creature of God how can you know Him and be close to Him! Developing the pure love of God in your heart can take away all fears from your mind. There are some people who are hoping for someone to arrange their salvation, while God is right here to give them salvation. That is what the great prophets and teachers came here to teach.

When you love God, sky is not the limit but the starting point

Our behavior is such as if we are not interested to listen to God and obey His commands. We want that He should forgive us when we make mistakes and provide us salvation. We can do whatever we like as we have so many things to do in this world; we have no time for God! Actually, we are looking for short-cuts.

Other people are focused on good deeds and they are afraid of negative deeds so as to avoid punishment. God forgives them as He has promised that He would forgive yet they continue asking

Him for forgiveness. Due to lack of spiritual knowledge, they do not realize that God wants them to move forward but they still keep asking for what they have already been given. They do not understand.

This goes on until they leave this world and discover in the next world that they have lower ranks. They were supposed to follow the path of love so that they could have been on the highest level of paradise in the presence of God along with those God has brought near.

This fear is an emotion which is negative and prevents people from soaring higher. However, love or ishq is a positive emotion which can take you above the heavens. When you are driven by love, sky is not the limit but the starting point. The result is that you will be in the Presence of God here as well as in paradise. You have the opportunity to achieve a total success and a great transformation of life!

When you love God, paradise is at your feet

63

Excellent Character and Actions

"Is not the result of excellent actions, excellent rewards."[190]

"To each one is a rank according to the deeds which he does."[191]

God wants to see who is best in character, actions and deeds. There are good deeds and then there are excellent actions.

Your relationship with God determines the quality of your actions

Your knowledge and relationship with your Creator guide you to high-quality deeds and actions and helps you build excellent character over time. A seeker with the foresight, knowledge and wisdom likes to engage in excellent actions.

"You pray as if you are seeing God. If you cannot feel that way, then you imagine that God is seeing you." [192]

Money and wealth are never loyal to anyone. They come and go. I have seen on television millionaires crying because they lost all their savings due to the financial scandals and economic melt-down. God's bounties and favors are with you all the time if you love and serve Him. Your physical beauty will gradually show the effects of age with the passage of time. There comes a time when you will see your self in the mirror and realize that time has gone by so fast.

Only the love of God becomes more intense and enduring with the passage of time. Love never leaves you. Your good deeds are permanently with you. Your inner beauty makes you feel young and beautiful all over and your outer beauty becomes radiant.

Through love and passion for God, you can develop excellent character. You will serve God and your fellow human beings and thus live a life of excellence.

The True Wealth

"Your true wealth is the good deeds which you do in this world."[193]

God has given riches and bounties for your comfort, enjoyment and to share with those who are less fortunate. You work hard so you have every reason to use and enjoy your possessions but those possessions should not make you neglectful of the remembrance of your loving Creator, appreciation of His favors and ignoring the unfortunate ones.

God asks us to do business with him which is everlasting and that multiplies your wealth too. That business is generosity in spending part of your wealth on those who are less fortunate, and investing in projects that benefit mankind through medicine, hospitals, schools, learning centers, and shelters. Whatever you will spend to uplift less fortunate and the poor should come back to you multifold. This is the business of prosperity without any loss.

One should encourage great deeds like helping and feeding the poor and orphans, giving clothes and shelter to the homeless and uplifting them, helping victims, visiting the sick, teaching the poor, fasting, being patient and forgiving others.

If one wishes to please God, then he should avoid negative thoughts, habits, and actions like jealousy, pride, boasting, bragging, arrogance, greed, anger, envy, hatred, injustice, oppression, violence, murders, unnecessary wars and hoarding of wealth and property while others around you are suffering.

You can learn from the Prophet's alchemy:

"Whatever God gives you, be content."[194]

At the very moment you become content in affliction, the doors of affluence and paradise will open. If the messenger of heartache comes to you, embrace him like a friend! Bestow a warm welcome on a cruelty that comes from the Beloved. Don't complain about hardships and subdue your self. You will be surprised to see the unexpected generosity extended to you and all your problems resolved favorably.

A smile is a charity. [126]

The Prophet Muhammad said that a smile is a charity and even earning income for yourselves and your families is a kind of worship. It is better to engage in honest work, business, and trading or fulfill the rights of your families, relatives, friends, orphans and community. He inspired them to engage in the worship, remembrance and contemplation in God and in helping and serving others.

Become a model with noble habits and excellent character

64

God can come into a Believer's Heart

"My heavens and My earth encompass Me not, but the heart of My gentle, believing and meek servant does encompass Me."[195]

The Heart is the perfect mirror that can reflect the true beauty.

Man's task in this world is to cleanse his heart, to polish it, and ultimately turn it into the house of God.

The ultimate center of man's consciousness, his inmost reality, his "meaning" as known by God, is called the heart. As for the lump of flesh within the breast, that is the shadow or uttermost skin of the heart. Between this heart and that heart are infinite levels of consciousness and self-realization.

The heart of the seeker "contains" God, while the heart of the ordinary man is mired in water and clay.

The worth of a man is determined by the state of his heart.

Most men are veiled by innumerable levels of darkness, so that in practice the center of their consciousness or heart is their ego. It is not pure enough for a reflection of God's beauty. Man's inmost reality, the heart, is always with God. But only the prophets and seekers, who are called the possessors of the heart, have achieved intense God consciousness. They are truly aware of God and all good qualities dwell in their hearts.

The Rumi's expression of love in the heart:

The house of the heart that remains without illumination from the rays of the Magnificient Sun.

Is narrow and dark and empty of the Loving King's sweet taste
The Sun's light does not shine in that heart,
Space does not expand, doors do not open,

You can make the door to the King's palace through the heart.

Come into the heart, the place of contemplating

This world is but a guest house.
Though it is not so now, it can be made so.
Close down speech's door and open up the heart's window!
The Moon will only kiss you through the window.

Once the Mirror of your heart becomes pure and clear, you will see pictures from beyond the domain of water and clay.

Not only the picture but also the Painter,
How should the orients of the lights of God Almighty
Be contained in the heart?

Yet when you seek His Light,
You find it in the heart,
Just as you find your own picture in the mirror,
Though your picture is not truly contained by it.

But when you look into the mirror,
you see yourself.

The seekers have polished their breasts until cleansed of greed, cupidity, avarice and hatred. Without doubt the pure Mirror is the heart acting as a receptacle for infinite pictures. Know that the heart's mirror has no limits. Here the intellect must remain silent or else lead us astray. For the heart is with Him indeed, He is in the heart

Through God's perfect power the bodies of spiritual men have gained the strength to bear the ineffable light! Hence the seal of the Prophet Muhammad related a saying from the eternal and everlasting King:

"I am not contained in the heavens and the earth. Yet I can come in the believer's heart, without qualification, definition or description." [196]

Outside of the seven heavens, greater than the two worlds!
And this is wonderful: that loving one is hidden within the heart!

If the seven heavens are too narrow for Him, how does He enter my heart? If the two worlds were to enter my heart, they would be contemptible. What a wonderful expansion thou hast given my wounded heart through **Thy love**!

Rumi

The heart is nothing but an ocean of light. Is the heart to be the locus of God's vision and then blind?

Heart is where the attributes of God and His essence are manifested after your heart has been purified and saturated with His love.

65

God's Essence and Magnificent Attributes

A distinction is made between God or the divine essence and God as He describes Himself in a revelation. In the Quran, He-calls Himself by many names such as the merciful, the all knowing, the living, and the all-powerful. From these names, we understand that He possesses the attributes of Mercy, Knowledge, Life and Power. But what is God's Essence?

"God is the Light of the Heavens and the Earth."
197

The Prophet Muhammad advised us to contemplate in God's attributes and His essence. Further, he informed us **not to investigate God's physical Essence.**

That which can be conceived concerning His essence is not in reality His essence. Since you have not the endurance for His essence, turn your eyes toward the attributes. Since you do not physically see the directionless, behold His light in the directions.

God's Essence and His attributes

God's attributes can be divided into two categories: the attributes of the essence and the attributes of the acts. The first category of names consist of the attributes of the essence like God is the living, the powerful, and the all-seeing. The second category is the attributes like He is kind, forgiving and bestower of favors.

The distinction between the essence and the attributes of God is purely conceptual, in the sense that there is no logical difference between the two sides. But in creation, these two attributes can be manifested through an infinite variety of forms.

The man veiled from the attributes sees His handiwork, while he who has got sight of the essence is with the attributes. Those who have attained closeness to Him are drowned in the essence.

Rumi says:

"Consider the creatures as pure and limpid water, within which shine the Attributes of the Almighty.
Their knowledge, their justice, and their kindness—all are stars of heaven reflected in flowing water.
Kings are a locus of Manifestation for God's Kingliness, the learned a locus for His Knowledge.
Generations have passed, and this is a new generation. The moon is the same, the water different.

Justice is the same justice, learning the same learning, but peoples and nations have changed.

Generations upon generations have passed, O' friend, but these meanings are constant and everlasting.

The water in the stream has changed many times, but the reflection of the moon and the stars remains the same.

All pictured forms are reflections in the water of the stream: when you rub your eyes, indeed, all are He."

66

God's Spiritual and Material Acts

There are three basic levels of existence.

"Verily His are the Creation and the Command." [198]

Here creation refers to the physical creation, while command denotes the spiritual world, which is "from the command of thy Lord."

The divine love is the sun of perfection, its light is the command, and the creatures are as shadows.

Know that the world of command is without directions, Oh friend! Therefore the Commander is even more Directionless. Rumi

The intellect is without directions, and the teacher of the exposition of God is more Intellect than intellect and more Spirit than spirit. No creation is without connection to Him, but that connection is too sacred to be expressed in words.

After all you also see God at this very moment in His effects and acts. Every instant you see something different, for none of His acts resemble any other. The effects and the fruits of God's mercy are manifest, but who except Himself knows mercy's essence? No one knows any of the essences of His attributes of perfection except through their effects and through analogy.

To be able to perceive the essence is the state of the uncommon people; everyone cannot attain this. For essence, and the mystery of its mystery, are manifestly visible before the eyes of the perfect teachers. In the whole of existence, is there anything further from understanding and penetration than the mystery and essence of God? Since that does not remain hidden from His intimates, what essence and attribute can remain concealed?

67

The Invisible Veils over Reality

This world is like a mirage or a dream compared to the infinite after life

Great dominating empires of the past have disappeared from the world. Famous philosophers, kings, presidents, and great generals of the past era have gone to the next life. Once they ruled the world with their iron fists. Where are Alexander the Great and Julius Caesar now? Everything seems like a great dream.

The world has been created to be so wonderfully attractive and captivating that man gets lost in its various attractions and its traps. Our desires for the things of this world keep increasing and expanding endlessly. Humanity is engulfed in this mirage and we have abandoned God who loves us intensely. Review your past life and you will find that many years of your life have gone by like a dream or a movie. Look at the gorgeous hair and pretty face you had and now they are showing the effects of the passage of time.

Veils of illusions prevent us from seeing the truth and reality.

"When people die; (it is like) they wake up from their sleep."[199]

Due to the veils over our eyes, we are following the illusions that we believe to be the truth. A lot of people are living under the influence of illusions and are probably in darkness not believing in God.

People do not understand the true nature of this world; otherwise, their actions, behavior, and habits will dramatically change.

There is more that you do not see than what you see.

Only when a man leaves this world, will his eyes be opened to the veils of this world and the reality of the next world. He starts seeing things previously invisible and this new reality gives him an incredible shock. But the spiritual person has already seen the invisible things due to his relationship with God.

Spiritually speaking, the world is like a dream, a prison, a trap, or dust kicked up by a passing horse. But it is not what it appears to be. So what you are seeing in the material world is like **a veil over the reality**. You make your decisions in life based on the incomplete reality.

The true reality is that permanent things are invisible and temporary things are visible.

Permanent things are invisible and temporary things are all around us. Where is the paradise in which you live forever? Invisible. Where are Abraham, Moses, Jesus, Muhammad and the other great people before them? In paradise which is invisible. The world and all that you see around is like a dream or a mirage.

Form and meaning.

Form is a thing's outward appearance and meaning its inward and unseen reality. Ultimately, meaning is the thing, as it is known to God Himself. The outward form passes away, but the world of meaning remains forever.

The goal of all things is God.

Form is a shadow, meaning the Sun.

Rumi says:

"How long will you make love with the shape of the jug?
Leave aside the jug's shape: Go, seek water! God

Having seen the form, you are unaware of the meaning. If you are wise, pick out the pearl from the shell."

The world then is form or a collection of myriad forms. By its very nature each form displays its own meaning, which is its reality with God. It is man's task not to be deceived by the form. He must understand that form does not exist for its own sake, but manifests a meaning above and beyond itself.

People look at secondary causes and think that they are the origin of everything that happens. But it has been revealed to the seekers that secondary causes are no more than a veil on the eyes, for not every eye is worthy of seeing the secrets behind His craftsmanship.

One must have an eye that cuts through secondary causes and tears aside all veils. Whoever looks on secondary causes is for certain a form worshiper. Whoever looks on the primary cause has become a light that discerns meaning.

The world's forms are like foam upon the sea.

Rumi says:

"His beauty is the Sun, His veil the world
Dear one, look at the Painter!
Why do you stare at the pictures?
Light is the First Cause, and every secondary cause is its shadow."

We are all darkness, and God is light. We focus on Light to become light

From this point of view form is place and meaning is no place. He manifests Himself in place, but in truth He has no place. God and meaning exist while form and the world are temporary and nonexistent.

People who have surrendered and are close to God are aware of this world and the next. God keeps guiding and protecting them in this world and afterlife because of their devotion and love for Him.

This world has no value when you are in the other world.

When an infant is in the womb of his mother, he does not value this world. When a person is in this world, he does not even think of the life in the womb. When the person is in the next world, he knows that afterlife is the permanent life, and life in this world was just like a blink of an eye or a dream he saw during the night.

We should bring a Spiritual Revolution in our lives

The greatest wisdom then is to estimate the true value of this world and bring a spiritual revolution in our lives right here and now. God gives the seekers true wisdom and value of this world and the next world, so that they can become truly successful

We should discover the presence of God so close to us.

God is running the affairs of this universe each day and He is always present before us. He is watching us. He never sleeps, but we hardly have a few moments to reflect and meditate, and discover His beauty.

The Prophet Muhammad said that this world is a place of planting the seeds and the next world is the place of harvesting the crop. Further, he said you live in this world like a traveler who stopped at a station to rest and then continued his journey. Knowing this we should devote our time to the permanent things by bringing those who are living in darkness into light.

We should do great works that truly benefit mankind. We should develop great habits and excellent character. That is how we can bring a spiritual revolution in our lives

68

Be Aware of Thy Enemy: Satan

It is good to know the traps of Satan

Satan has no power but he whispers negative suggestions

to take mankind from light to the darkness.

"But he (satan) had no authority over them, except that we might test the man who believes in the afterlife from him who is in doubt concerning it? And thy Lord is protector of everything."[108]

God has created man and woman for the comfort and love of each other. Some couples have children whom they enjoy and take care of them just the way they were taken care of by their parents. That is how one generation lives and then passes the torch to the next generation. The peaceful family life is the blessing of God.

The following is an imaginary scene portrayed in Rumi's poetry:

The accursed Satan said to the Creator, "I want a mighty trap for hunting human beings." **God showed him gold, silver and herds of horses; and said:**

"You can steal away people with these but not my true servants."

Satan said, "Marvelous," and his lips dropped down morosely; he became shriveled and sour like a lemon. Then God gave that ill-starred Satan gold and jewels from wonderful mines. "Take these other traps, oh accursed one!" He said, "Give me more than this,

Oh best of Helpers!" He gave him sweet and rich foods, delicious drinks, and many garments of silk. He said, "Oh Lord, I need more help than this so that I can tie them with a rope of palm fiber.

Those who are intoxicated in Thy love and courageous can break these negative bonds.

O' King of the Throne, give me a snare treacherous in deception

Through these traps and cords of self-will, Thy men will be separated from the unmanly. I want other snares, O' King of the throne, a man-throwing snare, treacherous in deception."

God brought wine and tantalizing music and placed them before him; Satan smiled a bit and almost became happy. Then he called out to God's eternal attribute of leading astray:

"Stir up dust from the depths of temptation's ocean!"

So He showed him the beauty of a woman, greater than the intellect and patience of men. Satan snapped his fingers and began to dance with glee: **"Give her to me at once. I have attained my desire!"**

When he saw those languorous eyes that agitate the mind and the intellect, their cheeks' purity that throws the heart's incense into the fire. The face, the mole, the eyebrow, the carnelian lips, the hair...

> *God Himself seemed to shine forth from behind a delicate curtain.* [200]

Satan was now fully equipped to trap human beings and lead them astray from God. I call his traps, spiritual weapons of mass destruction to cause violence, depression, and wars. The famous example is the ancient story of the Helen of Troy and their wars.

Now Satan knows what trap he can use for which person or group of people. You can see so much killings going on in the world that does not make sense at all. Those, who are killing the innocent people, think they are doing a great deed but God is patiently watching and they will be held accountable. The Satan makes their evil deeds seem as virtuous actions. When one kills an **innocent** person, he is at war with his Creator because God is on the side of the innocent person. It is only a matter of time before he will have to give account of his actions.

But the men of God know all the tricks of Satan and he has no power over these men and women who put their deep trust in God, the best of all protectors.

Satan could not trap Jesus and Muhammad

In a dream, I met Jesus Christ. He was shown to me as being incredibly handsome and had long beautiful hair, and bright face He was wearing just one long white cotton gown and leather slippers. It appeared to me that he did not have any property, house, foods, horse or money. Compare that to what the religious people, who claim to represent him, have accumulated today! But he had more spiritual power than anyone at that time.

Once Jesus was resting on the ground with a large stone under his head as a pillow to rest. Satan said to Jesus, "now you are resting comfortably and enjoying yourself." Jesus took the stone from under his head and threw at Satan. He could not trap Jesus in any way.

The Prophet Muhammad said that everyone has his Satan with him. People asked: "what about you O' Prophet." He said: "God had given me control over Satan." He said that a believer with firm faith in God is harder to Satan than one thousand believers with weaker faith.

Acquisition of wealth is not a sin if we share it through charity

There is nothing wrong to acquire wealth and good things of life. But we should share wealth by helping family members and our fellow human beings. Invest wealth on building industries for poors and underprivileged. It will come back to you multi-fold. Wealth grows through charity.

When human beings adopt extreme positions and become violent towards innocent people, they too act like satan. What if someone takes drugs or drinks and drives killing innocent people? What about when a head of family kills his spouse, children and himself in a so-called murder suicide? This is the work of Satan.

A man of firm faith is never influenced by Satan.

Satan aims to cause rifts in the family lives. He has parties celebrating victories over human beings with millions of broken families. People killing each other in the name of something important and each side claiming God is on their side. In fact, God is the source of Peace and harmony.

There are abnormal cases when the men are following their passions Satan interferes to break marriages and family ties so that people are unable to focus in God and become hopeless. You can see a man and a woman loving each other, getting married, having children, enjoying a happy married life and then, all of a sudden, there is a swift separation, a divorce and a house broken. What happened to their love for each other. Could it be Satan whispering his ideas to cause the break-up. If you have close relationship with God, your married life will grow stronger. The satan also whispers various reasons in the minds of children to turn them against their parents.

The financial institutions sometimes act like the evil-doers. People come to me for advice or consultation due to the extreme pressures being exerted on them by the financial institutions. They drag people to courts. They drive people to commit suicides. There are thousands of examples. That is why people need faith and become close to God. No harm will come to them and they will be guided and protected. We should help each other to alleviate these issues.

When you have firm belief in God, the solution to every problem is waiting for you. Never give up my friend. Seek guidance from God.

69

Feeling the Presence
of God Within

They are like the secrets of
the Omnipresent God.

We possess attributes of nonexistence, and God Almighty possesses the superlative attribute of existence. Having no existence and existential attributes, we possess no activity of our own. God alone is active and the only Doer. No action can take place in the universe without the energy provided by the Creator.

The seeker now sees God alone is the living One, outwardly and inwardly. He alone is eternal, powerful, has knowledge of the visible and invisible and is the Hearer and the Seer. By this distinction of his "poverty" the seeker automatically gains the distinction of trust (Amanah); he begins to see that attributes and actions are manifested in him as a trust.

"And We presented the trust (Amanah) to all creations...no one accepted this trust but man accepted it."[201]

The seeker exists through the existence of God alone. He lives through His energy, knows through His knowledge, has power through His power, hears through His hearing, sees through His sight, and speaks through His speech.

"My servant continually seeks to win my favor by superior actions until I love him; and when I love him I am to him an ear and an eye and a hand and his feet. Through Me he hears and through Me he sees."

"I am to him a heart and a tongue, through Me he understands and through Me he speaks." [202]

70

The Universe Has Only One Controller

Everything is connected to its origin and Humanity is like one family in a great village.

The science is now discovering that the entire universe did not just happen and it cannot exist by itself. The universe has a system, balance, central command and control, and a wise Controller.

The force of love pulls you to the center.
The negative force takes you away from the center.
Hatred separates you, love harmonizes.

Through remembrance of God and contemplation, you can develop a deep state of **consciousness** that will enable you to live spiritually. You will find all human beings as one family through

One Creator. Everything in the universe is connected and there is only one controlling power, the Beloved God.

Now you can start seeking the blessed Face.

God says, "Where are you going?" [203]

You have been very patient up to this point. We are sure you have gained knowledge and developed love of God in your heart. This path of love does not stop you from living and enjoying the comforts of modern world. You do not have to put yourself through unnecessary suffering and hardship. You can sit in the comfort of your own home and become aware of His presence. You can become spiritually successful right where you are.

God is present with you and you too have to be present

The spiritual information detailed in this book can inspire you to experience transformation in your life, and you can realize your life's full potential spiritually and materially. God is always present with you, but you should become conscious and aware of His presence.

Glimpses of the blessed Face:

Faces of mercy, love, compassion, and forgiveness.

The blessed Face emanating so many different lights like the rainbow. The rays of light are shining all over the universe.

God can show us the face of His Mercy.
God can show us the face of His Love.
God can show us the face of His Light.
God can show us the face of His Compassion.
God can show us the face of His Power.
God can show us the face of His Wisdom.
God can show us the face of His Perfection.
God can show us the face of His Beauty and Majesty.
God can show us the face of His Healing
God can show us the face of His Purity
God can show us the face of His Justice
God can show us the face of His Honor
God can show us the face of His Generosity.
God can show us the face of His Joy.

God can give us a new life

God can guide us
God can see us
God can hear us
God can teach us
God can befriend us
God can give us knowledge
God can give us wisdom
God can communicate with us
God can heal us from sickness
God can feed us spiritually
God can quench our thirst spiritually
God can give us our best life

So that we can experience

The Light of Mercy
The Light of Compassion
The Light of Love
The Light of Wisdom
The Light of Peace
The Light of Faith
The Light of Healing

To the arrogant and those who foster corruption, commit violence, and use cunning and destruction on this earth, God can show the Face of His displeasure and anger just as he did to ungrateful and unbelieving nations in the past. He is always compassionate, merciful, full of pity, and forgiveness to those who believe and are grateful. It is better not to break the limits established by Him even though He is tolerant and patient beyond imagination

71

You Can Now Begin

A Spiritual Revolution in Your Own Life

Are you ready for your best life now?
nothing can stop you to reach heavens
The sky is the starting point

You can move forward and spiritually go beyond heavens. You can make this world and the next as your paradise. You can please God and He will be pleased with you.

You can live your best life now by knowing God
Love of God empowers you in all aspects of your life

That does not stop you from having a good life with your family, having a great job, doing business, serving in the government, studying science, making jets and taking your family for vacation to some resort. It is simple to focus and remember God while you are doing all your daily chores and investing some time in learning the spiritual values and love of God. You can still make progress in the worldly life. You have a decent house and everything you wanted to have. God wants you to live an honored and comfortable life guided by spiritual values and love for all humanity.

There is no need for fears, hatred, undue anger, revenge, and greed, passion for worldly acquisitions, jealousy, boasting, pride, violence, swearing, and malice. There is no need for losing control of your self. Anything, that can make you lose control of your self is negative and should be avoided because you get this gift of life only once.

Now let the Love of God empower you in all aspects of your life so that you can start living your best life. You will be successful in your life in this world and you will be rewarded a rank and a place in paradise beyond your expectation and imagination.

Reflect for a few moments. Take a deep breath and realize the presence of God close to you. Write down how you can intensify this spiritual feeling. How you can develop love, passion, and longing in your heart for your loving Creator and have compassion and love toward your fellow human beings? Aim to begin a spiritual revolution in your life.

On the basis of what you have learnt, write how you can realize your life's full potential and lead a successful life spiritually and materially. Refer back to the book, if necessary. You can establish a plan of action for your life's transformation based on what you have learnt in this book.

How you can make a positive difference spiritually and materially in your family, community, nation and and in the world

----

The Opening

(Guide me to the Straight Way)

In the Name of God, The Most Compassionate, the Most Merciful

All the praises and thanks to God, the Lord (the Cherisher and Sustainer) of all the worlds

The Most Compassionate, the Most Merciful

The Only Owner (Master and the Ruling Judge) of the Day of Resurrection

You (Alone) we worship, and You (Alone) we ask for help Guide us to the Straight Way

The Way of those on whom You have bestowed Your Grace,

Not the way of those who earned Your anger,

Nor of those who went astray.   Q1:1-7

The Kursi (the Divine Chair)

God! La ilaha illa Huwa (none has the right to be worshipped but He), The Ever-Living, the One Who sustains and protects all that exists. Neither slumber nor sleep overtakes Him. To Him belongs whatever is in the heavens and whatever is on the earth. Who is he that can intercede with Him except with His Permission? He knows what happens to them (His creatures) in this world, and what will happen to them in the Hereafter. And they will never compass anything of His Knowledge except that which He wills. His Divine Throne extends over the heavens and the earth, and He feels no fatigue in guarding and preserving them. And He is the Most High, the Most Great. Q 2-255

Index

Index

59.	Quran	121	89.	Q 2:256	183
60.	Shk Ahmed	121	90.	Q55:60	187
61.	Q32:34	121	91.	Q 2:255	190
62.	Prophet Muhammad's		92.	Q14:34	193
	prayer	123	93.	Q14:7	193
63.	Q6:103	125	94.	Q14:7	193
64.	Q50:16	128	95.	Q55:13	196
65.	Quran	131	96.	T.Qudsi	199
66.	T.Qudsi	132	97.	Q103: 1,2,3	199
67.	Q20:12	133	98.	Tradition	210
68.	Q20:14	133	99.	Quran	211
69.	T.Qudsi	134	100.	Quran	243
71.	Quran	137	101.	Q65:3	215
72.	Q50:16	137	102.	Q66:26,27	215
73.	Q 6:59	138	103.	Q13:28	221
74.	Q27:30	141	104.	T.Qudsi	221
75.	Q17:110	141	105.	Q 2:152	222
76.	Q27:62	142	106.	Q29:69	226
77.	T.Qudsi	145	107.	Q86:4	230
78.	Q39:53	145	108.	Quran	351
79.	Hadith Qudsi	145	109.	Q25:70	230
80.	Quran	149	110.	Q36:82	237
81.	Q22:18	161	111.	Quran	238
82.	Q24:41	161	112.	Q67:1,3	241
83.	Quran	162	113.	Quran	242
84.	Q32:17	162	114.	Q53:43	246
85.	Quran	165	115.	Q53:60	246
86.	Quran	171	116.	Q26:80	246
87.	T.Qudsi	174	117.	Q53:44	247
88.	Quran	177	118.	Q53:48	247

Qudsi tradition is a statement communicated to the Prophet by God
through the arch angel Gabriel

Made in the USA
Charleston, SC
19 August 2012